ALL TRUE, MAN
ALEXANDER O'NEAL

THE OFFICIAL AUTOBIOGRAPHY

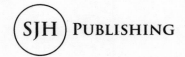
SJH PUBLISHING

For Cynthia

CHAPTER 1
Mississippi, goddam

Alexander O'Neal was looking forward to getting home. It was always hard working on the Mississippi and especially this time of year when it was just so darn hot and humid a man could hardly breathe. Hopefully, Dora would have supper on the table for when he got home. It was hard for her at the moment: little Pat round her feet all day and the pregnancy now so far along. If God was kind, he thought, hopefully they'd have a boy this time. Maybe he'd grow up to be a boatman like his father. It was a good job, government paid, and he knew he was lucky 'cos in Natchez it was hard for any black man, what with the way the whites were behaving. The Klan were active again, and God knows what troubles lay ahead.

Alexander turned back to his work. Probably another few hours to get this shipment of gravel off the boat and then he could call it a day. He headed inside the vessel to grab himself a cooling drink, still thinking about the times ahead, when the boat shifted to the side, slowly at first but then it suddenly flipped. The world turned upside down, water rushing in everywhere. Darkness.

Alexander was the father I never knew and after whom I was named. He died aged just 24, missing my birth by only a few months. All these years later, it still bothers me of the times we could have had, the role he would have played in my life, the guidance he would have provided in the times when life certainly threw its challenges at me.

Fate dealt me a tough hand from the start – born black and fatherless in the race-hate capital of the United States. Think pointed white hats, burning crosses and churches in flames – that's Natchez. We had our own resident Grand Dragon and, trust me, he wasn't like anything out of Harry Potter.

I grew up just before the civil rights movement of the 1960s really got going. The town was pretty much split in two – whites on one side, blacks on the other. We weren't called blacks then, nor African Americans. We were the word you can't use now, niggers, and the whites we addressed as massa. It was like you now see in the old movies, with separate schools, separate drinking fountains and separate tables in diners. It was one town but two different worlds.

My mother worked across town for a white lady, Miss Carr, as her maid. Miss Carr was a decent person, always treated my mother kindly, knowing it must be hard for her bringing up a family on her own. Because there was no father at home, Mom would often take me with her to help with the chores, cutting the grass or cleaning up the yard. I'd get paid $2, which I'd immediately give to Mom 'cos she needed every dime to make ends meet. On the way home across town though she'd always make sure to buy me a couple of hot dogs and a Coke.

Our home was nothing like Miss Carr's grand house. For families like ours, all we could afford was a place on Henderson Street. In reality, it was nothing more than a shack. After my father died, my mom had four other kids – Doris, Larrie, Brenda and Rita – all by different fathers. So there was a lot going on and little money to get by on.

However poor we were, though, there was never a speck of dust or dirt inside our house. We all had our chores during the week, and every Saturday was like a full spring clean with the whole place done from top to bottom. The only thing we had to contend with, like every family like ours, was the neverending battle with the armies of cockroaches and mice that always appeared at night. The noise of them running around the wooden floors kept me hidden under the covers on many an evening.

For me the biggest inconvenience in life was school. I wasn't the dumbest cat in the world, but I was intimidated by the material. Football, American style, was the only thing that interested me. I was great friends with the school quarterback, Ronnie Robertson, but it hadn't started out like that. Ronnie had two brothers, Renard and Pedo, who used to bully all the kids in the neighbourhood. I remember one Saturday morning I came out of the store with my brother, Larrie, and they started picking on us again, but this time I wasn't going to let them have it their own way. Bang, I hit one brother in the face then the next and finally me and Larry were going at it big time with me cussing, "You motherfucker, you been running me for a long time. I'm gonna to kick your mother-fucking ass."

It's the sort of language I've used all my life and, on this occasion, I was swearing so much that one of the neighbours, Miss Doll, came across while we were fighting and started shouting that she was going to tell my mother about my cussing. Sure enough, when I got home Miss Doll was telling Mom everything – but not in the manner I was expecting. "Alex whooped their ass today," she told my mom. "He whooped their ass!" She knew they were bullies and I'd been right to teach them a lesson.

While Miss Doll clearly cared about kids, most of the teachers at school – all black, of course – didn't really care, as far as I could see. This is especially true of the teachers who would disappear at lunch time and come back to class in the afternoon stinking of booze. Not very inspirational. I remember one particular teacher, Miss Mock, who was an absolute monster, and one of the nastiest, meanest people I have ever encountered. Her particular way of encouraging us was to scream, "You guys are pathetic." When you're a young kid, and you've got a raging adult screaming in your face, you just close up shop. All interest in anything they've got to say goes straight out the window.

In the few teachers and classes I was interested in, there was the other fundamental problem in that no one had ever actually taught me how to study. It's okay for the teacher to stand there in front of the class talking about the subject of the day, but if you are unable to interpret that into some sort of coherent answer, what's the point? Asking for help was not an option. I was afraid to even ask teachers anything because you were going to get embarrassed. They wouldn't take you with love and say, "O'Neal, come here. Come on outside, son. Let me talk to you." No. They was going to embarrass you in front of the whole class. That was their way of keeping you in check

Because I could play football, though – and this was the time of black affirmative action – I knew the school was going to graduate me even though I never even turned up for half my senior year. My mom would go to work in the morning, while I would get up and pretend I was going to school. When she took off, I would go right back to bed. I had it down to a fine art.

When I was at school, the teachers they had shit attitudes. They didn't take time to get us prepared. They kind of just whisked us straight through. You get enough grades, just enough, then you are going to graduate – even though you're not actually prepared or equipped to go to college.

When I left for college, I'd been at school for 12 years and really didn't know anything, and sadly I still didn't know how to ask for help.

Outside of school and as I approached my teens, the whole world seemed about to explode. This was the mid-1960s and Martin Luther King and Malcolm X were the names on everybody's lips. The blacks in Natchez, like our brothers and sisters all over the South, had decided enough was enough – we wanted an equal share in the life that the whites had taken from us.

For me, the years after slavery had to be more horrific than being in slavery. Had to be. Because every time you tried to be free, they showed you that you wasn't, and if you tried to insist on being free, then they would insist that you'd have to die. If you insisted on equality, then in the 1950s and 1960s, you got to die. That was the whites' only answer to the question. They'd come to get you out of your bed in your neighbourhood any time they wanted to. And who is going to defy it, strike back? You? You're black people. If you kill a white person, then they'd kill all of you.

The Ku Klux Klan was more active than ever at this time. I remember us all being in school one day and there must have been 25 cars full of Klansmen who just drove slowly by the school. Shit, they thought they were frightening us and at times before, they were right, but now the time when we were just going to sit back and take it was over. No matter what the intimidation, the struggle would not be stopped.

I remember one time we were marching down Main Street demanding something, I can't remember exactly what, when I saw this white woman come out of one of the shops and she squirted something right into the face of a black woman a few yards ahead of me. The woman fell to the floor, screaming in agony, her face ruined by the acid burning into her flesh. The whites just stood there saying nothing and the police were immobile as some of our marchers tried to help their screaming colleague.

Things got even worse as the civil rights revolution gathered pace.

A few doors down from where we lived was a good friend of my mother's, Wharlest Jackson. He'd come to Natchez after serving in the Korean War and had married a local girl, Exerlena, with whom he had five kids. Wharlest worked for a local company, Armstrong Tire and Rubber, and had done so well that he was promoted to a foreman's job, a role not normally given to blacks. For some of the whites in Natchez, this was the final straw. They already knew Wharlest was active in the civil rights movement, in fact he held a senior position in the NAACP, the National Association for the Advancement of Colored People.

I was at home one night with the family when suddenly outside we heard this enormous explosion. My mother begged me to stay inside, but like any kid my age, I had to go and see. It was a sight that has haunted me until this day.

Wharlest had been driving down the street coming back from work when a bomb planted in his Chevrolet detonated. Bits of the car were blown into homes either side of the street. Wharlest himself was blown to pieces – I could see his torso hanging wrapped around a telegraph pole. To this day his killers have remained undiscovered. There was suspects and investigations but, for Wharlest and many other fighters like him, there has never been the justice they deserve.

As the civil rights years marched on, things did start to improve – but only slowly. At school I met my first white friend, James McKnight, whose father owned a carnival. James used to come to my house and have dinner, red beans and rice and fried chicken. We'd hang out, smoke weed and run around and laugh and drink alcohol.

James had the weirdest sense of humour and that's what I loved about him. One day he took me out into the country, into places where only white people lived and where I'd never been before. We're going down this rocky road and he was driving like a maniac when he suddenly pulled up at this huge barn. "Open the door boys, I'm bringing 'em in!" he shouted, as if the Klan were waiting inside. This was the sort of place where they would kill you and bury you in the woods and nobody would find you. He just wanted to fuck with me and see the reaction on my face.

When I turned 18, and despite my academic performance, I was offered an athletic scholarship to Alcorn State University in Lorman, about 30 miles from home. My job was to play football, as a linebacker to be precise. At high school I'd been the cock of the walk, the football star, the good-looking young black man everyone wanted to be around.

To say I was unprepared was the understatement of the century. I thought I'd be on my way, be the college star and then the next step fulfil my dream of being a professional football player. God, as we now know, had other plans.

At Alcorn they took an entirely different attitude to the academic side of my life. Sure, I could play football but at the same time I had to put in the work in in the classroom as well, which wasn't the story back at high school.

English was the only subject I had any interest in, and the rest was a mystery to me. Algebra, geometry, that stuff was for the smart guys. Multiplication I could do but fractions and division – forget it. Pretty soon I was doing the bare minimum amount of work. The truth is I wasn't equipped to do it. I didn't want to do it. All I wanted to do was go to practice, go to lunch and come back to my room and go to sleep, get up and go to practice again. I didn't want to do the classes.

In my frustration, as the teachers pressured me over my grades, I quit the football team, which meant giving up on college. This was a huge decision that the team's coach knew could affect my whole life. He sat me down and managed to talk some sense into me. I'd give it another go but first off there'd be a price to pay for turning my back on the team. That could not go unpunished.

If you've ever seen American football, you'll know that it's a hard game. We don't pull punches. My punishment for the "betrayal" of quitting was to tackle the entire 50-man squad, one at a time. I knew the punishment would be tough, but 50 guys! I was a linebacker so I was built for speed and running round people, not getting smashed in the tackle every few minutes. Larry Campbell, my hero from high school, offered to take my place for me but the coach wouldn't hear of it. In fact he warned everyone that, if they took it easy on me, they'd take my place. It was a long afternoon and they wiped the floor with me.

It wasn't long though before the same issues that had led me to quit the team had piled up again. I couldn't do the book stuff and was never going to. Time to walk away before they threw me out. I quit Alcorn and switched to Copiah-Lincoln Community College just outside Natchez. I was happier being at home 'cos I'm a town boy at heart. Alcorn, man, was out in the woods and it sort of freaked me out.

Other than this being the first time in my life that I was at the same place where white kids were studying, the switch of college didn't really change much.

Sure I made the football team – I was good, honestly. The book work was the mountain I could never climb. At Copiah-Lincoln if you didn't make the grades you're off the team, simple as that. The only way to keep going was to have taken extra classes that I'd have to pay for and there was no way on the planet my mother could afford to do that.

My school days and my dreams of football stardom were over. Life had suddenly become very complicated. At home, things had also become difficult. In my time at high school and college I had a girlfriend, Avis Washington, who was my first love. We had sex a few times but in no way was I prepared for a proper relationship. I was also abusive and aggressive towards her, slapping her around whenever I got angry. Unfortunately, this behaviour was to follow me through my life, through marriages and girlfriends.

Down South in the 1950s, 1960s and 1970s it was okay, we thought, for white men and black men to slap their women around. On several occasions, I'd go to a friend's house and see the father have a fight with the mother and then slap her up. Eventually, I overcame that, but it took a long time. Basically every relationship I had my mother used to always tell me, "You're never going to keep a woman by beating her." She used to tell me that. It took me a long time to ask myself the question, "How can you love somebody yet beat them and hurt them?"

Every marriage I was in, I lost it because of that. Avis was the first relationship I lost. When we broke up, I later heard she said she had fallen pregnant by me. I don't know if that is true but, if it is, I would welcome it. The child, a boy, would be nearly 50 now, so it may be too late.

With all this going on it was time to get out of Natchez,

to do something with my life. Just what it would be only time would tell.

I would be heading out into the world as a young man who had pretty much set his own rules on how to behave and how to treat other people.

Something that I think affected me the whole of my life was the absence of my father – a role model who could teach me right from wrong. Without him, I grew up respecting no one.

I don't think any man, other than your father, has a right to tell you shit. I didn't have a father, but I had available role models like my grandfather and could take or leave what they said. It didn't mean anything to me 'cos I'm already fucked up in the head, thinking "There's nothing you can do 'cos you ain't my father."

Just the idea of not being able to ever know your father did some fucking mental shit to me. This is secret shit I carried with me. You had no one to talk to about it, your mother didn't explain shit to you and there was no one to get all these feelings and emotions out to. I didn't have that. I just had me and my little country Mississippi mind with which to deal with the world. For a long time, it wouldn't be enough.

CHAPTER 2
Heading north

O ut of college, I had to find a job and quickly as there was no way my mother could afford to have me lying around at home. An opportunity came up to train as an electrician, but it meant moving down to Jackson County and the town of Pascagoula. I swapped one small town for another and after six months knew this small-town living was never going to be the life for me. Inside I knew God had a plan for me that I'd have to find for myself, no matter how long it took. So I said goodbye to Pascagoula and, like millions of other blacks from the South, I headed for the North.

In Chicago was my uncle, Walter O'Neal, who was my father's only brother. I'd just turned 19 and knew nothing about life, nothing at all. Walter lived on the west side of the city, which was where most of the black community was based. He agreed to put me up in his basement flat and within a week helped find me work at an aluminium factory, loading and unloading supplies. When I got my first week's pay cheque for $125 I thought, shit, this is a whole load of money, more than I'd ever seen at home – I'm on Easy Street. That's when I learned my first lesson of trying to stand on my own two feet because Walter wanted $75 rent, which left me with just 50 bucks to live on.

In a lot of ways, life in Chicago was like it had been at home. The black community kept to themselves. There were no Kluckers – what we called the Ku Klux Klanners – around, but the racial divide was as wide as it had ever been Down South. After a year living with my uncle in a deadbeat job, I knew I had to move on again. There had to be an adventure out there somewhere.

In Minneapolis, I had a cousin, Cornell Washington, and I rang him to see if he could put me up. Sure, he said, and that same night I was on a Greyhound bus on my way to Minnesota. My first sight of Minneapolis the following morning took my breath away. Remember, I'd come from the Deep South to the West Side of Chicago. Minneapolis was like nothing I'd seen before.

When I arrived at Cornell's apartment building, it seemed beautiful, and I remember thinking it looked like something you'd see on TV, but for white people, not somewhere blacks would live. Cornell was out at work, and I was amazed when the building's supervisor appeared and, after explaining who I was, invited me to dump my things in his apartment until Cornell returned. I'd a few hours to kill so I decided to take a walk. There was a small lake nearby, and I was walking around it when this guy appeared and we started talking. Shit man, the next thing I knew he was rolling us both a joint and we're sitting on the grass shooting the breeze. It was like I'd died and gone to heaven. Minneapolis was a place where I knew I could finally relax, be myself and do my own thing.

Minneapolis had another massive surprise for me – blacks and whites lived together, in the same apartment buildings, in the same streets. For the first time, I saw white girls with black men, black girls with white men. The only time I'd ever seen anything like it was watching *Shaft* on TV, the only black guy who got to make love to a white girl. In Natchez or Chicago's West Side, such a thing was unthinkable. At first, I wasn't ready to accept such a change in mindset. It took me time to understand that interracial relationships teach people things they don't know about. For me – and many other black Americans – we had more problems coming to the party because of the black hatred that had become ingrained in us by a lifetime of oppression.

First things first, though: what was I going to do? I naïvely thought about trying to get a trial with the local football team, the Minnesota Vikings but, to be honest, I didn't have the balls to pick up the phone and make the call. Instead, I ended up pumping gas at Super America, at least I was earning money, enough to get by. I remember one time this car pulled in and in the back was this whole pile of drums. I asked the driver how he'd got into music, and he explained a few things. His name was Bobby Vandell and years later he was the drummer in my band.

My cousin introduced me to his friends, and we'd go to bars and clubs and stuff, but it felt like black girls didn't like me. Pumping gas, shit man, if you didn't have a car and stuff they'd have shit to do with you.

God had another surprise in store for me though when I met a white woman who lived in another apartment in Cornell's building. Her name was Barbara Coleman and she had a young son who lived with her. We hit it off and before long I'd moved out of Cornell's flat and set up home with Barbara.

Barbara was a lovely woman, and we stuck it out for about two or three years, but it was like riding a rollercoaster. When we argued she was not the kind of woman who would stand there and let me slap her around, she'd fight back, even if I'd do most of it. With her son, I think I was too much out of Mississippi to be a father to him. I couldn't do it, and I suspect it was that "black racism" thing which still burned in me, despite the fact I lived with a white woman.

In September in Minneapolis, the snow starts to fall and, in that weather, a boy from Mississippi doesn't want to be standing outside all day pumping gas. I quit my job and switched to a bakery where I worked in the loading bay, but that was also only going to be short-term. The plan I'd worked out was get enough money together so that I could travel to Wisconsin where I'd found somewhere that would help me get my trucker's licence. Good money in trucking and, but for a twist of fate, that could have been my life.

Back home in Natchez, Mom used to take us to church every Sunday where the preacher would rant and rave about the eternal damnation waiting on all us poor sinners. When he wasn't preaching and we weren't praying the whole congregation would be singing. I didn't think anything of it at the time but I had a voice, seemed everyone but me knew I was really good. I remember at school when I was about nine a teacher, Miss Colreen, used to offer me a dime if I'd sing the old gospel song, "Steal Away". My first paying performance.

At college, too, the guys used to try and get me to sing. I remember blowing them away one time doing my take on "Where Is The Love", that classic by Roberta Flack and Donny Hathaway. At one point before college, I even dabbled in a band I set up with my friend Mike Mackle, whose family owned a funeral parlour in Natchez. Naturally, we called ourselves The Soul Morticians, but I didn't even know what mortician meant. We were about 14 at the time, me up front singing with Larry Harris and Tony Lucas, Mike on bass guitar and three guys on horns. Saturday nights we'd perform at The Catholic Hall to about 100 screaming kids as we blasted out stuff from the likes of James Brown and the Righteous Brothers – really good soul stuff. Everybody, all the people from school and stuff, would come to our show. Mike's dad took whatever money he collected on the door, the rest of us never got a quarter.

Other bands would try to get me to sing with them, but I never would. I wasn't used to working with older musicians who were playing in clubs. They wanted me to sing with them, but I didn't want to do it because some of the guys were gangsters. They were bullies, too.

There's one guy named Big Jack. I'll never forget Big Jack. Big Jack wanted to pick me up off a street corner one day and go sing with his band. I didn't want to because I'd heard that Big Jack would bully his musicians to play. If he didn't like something you're doing, he might jump on you. He might snap you or something.

I didn't want to put myself in that kind of position, so I refused.

These were all long forgotten memories when, one morning, I'm out of the apartment in Minneapolis riding my bike through the neighbourhood park when I recognized this guy walking towards me. He was Bill Clark – one of the singers who'd been in a really good R&B band, The Philadelphia Story (they'd previously been called The Valdons). God knows what got into my head, but I jumped off my back and said to him, "Hey man, when's the last time someone told you they had a great voice and then showed you it was true?"

Bill just looked and me and smiled, saying nothing.

"Hey man, I can sing something for right now. Listen."

What a way to get an audition. I got off my bike, and I started singing. "Where is the love/you said you'd give to me/soon as you were free/will it ever be?"

It was the same song I sang to the guys at college. I was Donny Hathaway back in those days, right? You have certain people you mimic, certain people you try to sing like. Donny Hathaway was the guy who I tried to sing like, and could. When he heard me, Bill Clark was so impressed. He said, "Come on down to the club tonight."

Bill was now in a group out of Detroit called The Store Front Band and that night they were playing at the Flame Bar on Nicollet Avenue, which was on the southern edge of Downtown Minneapolis. On stage that evening they were supporting David Ruffin who had been one of the lead singers of The Temptations. Bill arranged for me to open the show with three songs. Now this was going to be a world of difference to a Saturday night in a church hall. I had decided before I went out that when I went on stage, I would look over the crowd, not directly at people's faces, which shows just how little I knew of how to work the stage.

I certainly looked the part – green flower-patterned polyester shirt, beige Sansabelt flares and giant platform shoes. Out I went, and I did my little three songs, and I went down a storm. Out there on stage, I made up my mind right then that this was what I wanted to do in my life. There was nothing else like it. The truck driving could wait. I gave myself ten years to land a record deal and if I hadn't done it by then, I probably never would.

That night also taught me what else success on stage in a club could bring – girls. The whole nine yards.

In Minneapolis, if you're a musician or a singer, and the Lord knows you to be good, well, you're going to start to notice a lot of female attraction. I had Barbara and her son back in our apartment, but I felt what happened outside, with other girls, was my business and nothing to do with her. I would be like this with her and other women for years to come until I learned that you could not behave like that.

While I knew where I wanted to go, it was a long time after my debut at the Flame Club that the singing started to take off. In the meantime, I needed money – proper money, not just the small pay packets I'd earn from little, part-time jobs. The experience of all those women throwing themselves at me was like a drug. I wanted more but, if I'm running around with hardly any money on me, they'd never look at me.

I never imagined in Natchez playing football that just a few years later I'd be breaking the law, going over the line to get the money I wanted. The scene I fell into was all about hustling. Hustling in everything that you do. I've been a stick-up man, a burglar, a hustler. Sometimes people mistake hustling and pimping. I wouldn't want to be a pimp. I really wouldn't want that job, because that's too much work. Pimping is something where you've got to keep people in line, you've got to check your girls all the time, you're the overseer. I wouldn't want no job like that.

So, hustling, it's not about owning somebody, it's about them doing what they want to do for you. It's just like a rich woman that wants to take care of a guy. You see it on TV. You see it in movies all the time. A rich woman wants to take care of a young guy. In Minneapolis and Saint Paul, everybody knew that money, hustling, and whoring around was a part of Twin Cities culture. I'd have a string of women who I could lean on for money.

For example, I'd visit one of my girls and show her I had a stash of, say, $2,000 on me but I needed to borrow another $3,000. She'd want to do anything she could to keep me happy and would give me the money, believing I'd be good to pay it back 'cos look, I've got a stash already, so she believes I'm making money. All the time, though, I'm playing with her and another girl's money, never my own.

I ain't proud of what I did but, at this time in Minneapolis and with the people I was running with, this is what we did. I don't know if I met the wrong people. I think it's more that they were the right people for me at that time. Everyone knew that money, hustling and whoring around was part of our culture. In New York at the time I'd say three-quarters of the women on the streets were from Minneapolis or Saint Paul. Shit, people used to come out from the New York to recruit girls to take back.

When I wasn't hustling, there was always another way to get some money. One of the easiest was holding up white drug dealers. Me and this one guy who was kind of my partner would deliberately put ourselves in situations where we could meet these dealers, get them to the point where they thought we were their friends and felt comfortable inviting us to their homes. These people were gullible. You invite us into your house as a dope dealer, and we'd case the joint and come back and stick you up. We'd go in masked, with a piece, the whole nine yards.

We were both big guys and muscular. You'd look at the two of us together and think, no way are you going to fuck with that. We would intimidate these guys so much – sometimes it was horrific. If someone has got a gun in your face and has already pistol-whipped you, then you're going to play ball. I never hit anyone 'cos I was in control but my partner, on the other hand, felt the need to pistol whip them and stuff like that. That was the way he did things. I didn't do things like that. Nobody ever got shot, thank God, but some serious stuff went down.

I remember this one time we went to rob some dope boys.

Some people we knew had set them up, telling us where the guys lived and that they'd probably have a load of drugs in the house. When we went round there one of the guys opened the door like an idiot. I tied them up like fucking Christmas trees while my guy held a .45 on them. My partner asked the guys if they had guns in the place and one of them had said no. He then started searching the whole place and, as he did so, he found this long-assed gun under the couch. Oh man, why did they lie? My friend proceeded to beat the guy who'd said "no" around the head with his .45. I had to stop him because the guy was passing out. I said, "Man, you're going to kill him." The last thing we needed was a murder rap on our hands. That was a bad scene that day. We got everything we came to get but that one lie nearly cost that boy his life. It really did.

Later, when we divided up the goods, I'd thought we'd gone there just to get weed, which there was quite a lot of, but there was also cocaine in there as well. I knew what it was, but I never wanted to have any of it because the people I'd seen using it very often would shoot it, inject themselves. I didn't want anything to do with that kind of shit. My partner, who was a little older than me, did have a lot of experience with cocaine. I told him he could keep the stash of cocaine, which I wanted nothing to do with it. His eyes must have lit up like it was Christmas time.

"Keep it all?" he said.

"Keep it all, dog," I replied. "I just want the jewellery, the money and the marijuana."

The package of cocaine must have been worth up to $10,000. Crazy.

We usually only went after people like these, dope boys. If they're making fast money from the street, they can lose it fast.

We were as bold as brass. Another time we invited these dope guys over to a house. They turned up with about two kilos of marijuana, everyone being friendly and all that when I ran in and robbed them all. The dope boys never had a clue my guys were all in on it from the start.

I don't have any remorse about robbing these guys, no more so than I guess they ever had for selling the stuff. We were living in the same world. They made their living selling drugs – I made mine taking that money off them.

However, when it came to burglary, I have to confess that nice people's homes went down, too, not just the bad guys. Everybody goes down with the burglar. I can see now that breaking into someone's home is a violation, something that people can struggle to come to grips with.

You never know how humiliating something like that is until it happens to you. It's an invasion of your privacy. It's almost as bad as getting raped or something. How do you get over some shit like that? You don't just get over that kind of thing. When someone breaks into your house, you don't really want to lay your head there.

I can only say at the time, aged 21 or 22, everything I did seemed right for me. It had a reason. The people I was with were the right people for me to be with at that point in time. I never wanted to hurt someone, but some people did get hurt.

At this period in my life, coming out of the Deep South where all I'd experienced was the oppression of blacks by whites, I was so red, black, and green – so into the idea of black liberation – that I couldn't even see straight. When I went to Minneapolis, I had a lot of love but also a lot of hatred inside me for white people. Period. I didn't want to hate, but the things that I was dealing with made me.

I was also learning a different kind of racism. I knew the kind of people Down South are right up in your face. You know where they stand. Up North, I had to get adjusted to their kind of racism. That kind of racism is this – they'll laugh in your face and stab you in the back like a motherfucker.

In the North, they pretend like they're friends, like they're all liberal, like they like you, but they still got their Confederates – when I saw some Confederate flags up North, I didn't really know how to take it. I didn't know. I was mortified. I was like, "Wow, these white motherfuckers."

It was like the white racists were saying, "Yes, we're every-where. We're every-motherfucking-where."

So, if you were going to come at me like that, and going to show me that, I'm going to keep my guard up. I'm not going to allow you to sucker punch me, slap me in the face, because I've got trust in you.

The reality was I was a black racist my damn self. White people think that they are the ones who hold the monopoly on racism. When you don't know, you don't have a clue.

People of colour hang on to racism as hard as white people do, even harder, because first of all, they are the victims of some dark racism. In return, we get the opportunity to spread that kind of shit all on each other. It's like crabs in a barrel. One black person going up you've got another to pull you right back down because they don't want you to go somewhere that they can't go. "If I can't go, then you can't go." That is horrible.

The reason why other races are so far past our racism is because we don't take care of each other. I don't care where we are. Whether we are in goddamn Africa, or we're in Jamaica, or we're in America, or we're in England. We just don't fucking take care of each other. That's the problem.

You look at the music industry. We don't take care of each other, but the white boys take care of each other. They still make it go around. Here's a scenario – you got a client like, say Tom Petty. Tom Petty wasn't the most talented motherfucker in the world. He was out there but he couldn't sing his way out of a paper bag. But Tom Petty still has worth. If he needed help, his Caucasian friends rally round and take care of him.

The Mexicans take care of each other, too. Look at them – they don't deal with the system, they do everything by themselves. They got their own credit union. They got their own banks. They have their own car lot. They got their own stuff.

Mexicans will work their asses off and won't complain. They won't say nothing about nothing. They just work. They're not going to say anything. They are going to get your money, because they're not used to having that. Once they get it, they know what to do with it. They take care of each other.

CHAPTER 3
Southern comfort

Living the way I did in those days, it was no surprise that eventually Barbara and I split up. We'd loved each other but just couldn't live together. We were too alike. God's plan, though, was not to leave me alone too long. Shortly after we broke up, I was on my bike one day going to work at the gas station on Franklyn Avenue when I bumped into this lovely girl, Evon Mills.

She was out walking her dog, a greyhound, and was as pretty as a picture. We hit it off instantly. Evon was only 17 or 18 but seemed to have her shit together. She was still at school, the Street Academy, which was for kids who couldn't make it in the public system. Evon had her own place, which really impressed me for someone so young. We dated, fell in love and, within a few months, we jumped into a marriage.

Not long after the wedding we had our first few rows and I slapped her. I thought it was natural and that she'd probably been hit by other guys before. It would still be a long time before I learned this abuse was so wrong and the worst thing in the world that you could do, but at the time I knew no better.

The time seemed right to take a break from Minneapolis, so Evon and I thought, okay, let's try going back to Natchez. It was a big mistake 'cos, after just a month, I knew small-town living was just not for me. I thought I'd try Jackson, the state capital of Mississippi, which I knew had its own great music scene with bands like the Wynd Chymes, the Freedom Band, Sho-Nuff and Dorothy Moore. Could be great, I've got Evon, the music and a lot of hustling on the side. After we had arrived in Jackson, I started hanging out with these guys and was helped by one of my homeboys, Forrest Gordon, who played with the Wynd Chymes. They'd already had a record deal with RCA, but it didn't last, and I think they may have been cut after just two albums.

It was just amazing being around all these great musicians, but incredibly they all still faced the problem of the inherent racism that still existed in the South despite all the advances of the civil rights movement.

Black bands in Jackson could play white venues if say, it was a festival or they'd been booked to perform at a private function like a wedding. But ordinary clubs on an ordinary night – no way. That would mean black boys and white girls and black girls and white boys in the crowd together, mixing like normal people. The whites in Jackson who owned most of the venues just weren't ready for this.

We played in the black clubs, but you're supposed to be able to play any place. You love my music, you love Otis Redding, you love James Brown but, in the 1960s, he can't play here no more. You can't play here because some white guy might not like it. Everything was still based on that. I swear to God.

It was the same sort of attitude at a place where I'd got a job working in a body shop fixing up cars. Remember I'd been up north in Chicago and out west in Minneapolis so I was not, for one second, going to stand for any overt racism whatsoever. The owner of the body shop, a white guy, he was impossible. He shouted over to me one afternoon just before I was due to finish my shift at four o'clock.

"O'Neal, you're working 'til seven," he screamed.

No fucking asking, just yelling his order. No fucking way, I thought.

"Absolutely motherfucking not," was my reply.

"What?"

He couldn't believe I'd answered him back.

"I said absolutely motherfucking not. Tell you what you can do – you can give me what motherfucking money I've got due, and I'm going to get the fuck out of here."

There was some hustling in Jackson and other times some of the friends I made would invite me to join them in more direct ways of making money.

One time one of them tried to get me to rob this white bar at closing time. I thought about it but decided hell no, I'm not going to do that. If you go in there with guns and shit, something could go wrong, and it would just be my luck for someone to get killed. What do I get then, life in prison in Mississippi? Fifty years?

This guy was desperate and volatile. You don't want to go into a robbery situation with a motherfucker like that, man. He was a friend of mine from college but I didn't want to take a chance on anybody who could lose the plot. Every time you go into a situation where you have guns, you take a chance on killing somebody. You don't carry a gun unless you are prepared to use it. A lot of times what happens is somebody goes on a robbery where they're not prepared to use the guns but end up doing just that, killing somebody inadvertently. Doesn't matter if you weren't the one pulling the trigger – you all go to prison for life. I had too much to offer, something inside of me, the way I was raised always made me go back to the good Alex, to the good person my mother raised. I walked away. Sure I needed money, but not this way.

In Jackson I soon got to know the bands more and, when they discovered I could sing, they'd invite me to join them on stage, particularly the Wynd Chymes, who would even take me on the road with them. They didn't want me as part of the actual band but they wanted me to be with them. They recognized how great my voice was and wanted me to open the show. Inadvertently they were teaching me a very valuable lesson. I believe no matter how good your band is, the lead singer *is* your band. Without a powerful lead singer you may be good, but that's all you are.

Jackson taught me how to put myself in a position to be needed. I didn't go in for the clothes and all that, or thought of myself as a pretty boy, but I knew I sure as hell was a motherfucker of a good singer and everybody wants one of those.

Charlie Wilson, a very good friend of mine from The Gap Band, would later tell me, "Boy, you got the strongest voice in the music industry."

Jackson also helped me to ask myself the question – how do I move to the next level? How do I exploit the gift that God had given me? What else to do but take what I'd learned in Jackson and go to Las Vegas, the entertainment capital of the world. Boy, was I in for a rude awakening.

I went out there to do music, and I figured I could go out there and be successful. For Evon it was always her dream for me to be a star, but it was not my dream at the beginning. Evon was the one who made me aware what I could be. She was smitten, like everyone around, with my voice. They couldn't believe there was this guy who could sing like this. I was half-ass interested and half-ass not. I was young and into my own things, getting high and smoking marijuana, chasing women, doing stuff like that.

First thing when we touched down in Vegas was to get a job and I quickly found a place working in a loading dock in Henderson which is about 15 miles south of the city. I had to get to work as best I could as Evon had to have the car for a little job she'd found. The money was shit and, alongside what I spent getting to and from work, it hardly left me anything at all, so it didn't take long for me to quit and go straight back to hustling.

Back in Minneapolis, for guys like me at that time, women were your number-one source of income. Sorry, but that's how it was.

This time around in Vegas it was more the gigolo kind of shit, not robbing and not pimping, which is not my thing. As I said, pimping is a hard job. You always got a girl running off on you and you got to keep everybody in line and how do you do that? Fear tactics. You don't keep them in line by saying, "Hi, how are you? I'm a really nice guy – you want to go out and make me a bunch of money?" No. It is tough, fear factor. I couldn't do anything like that. That just wasn't my cup of tea.

Now, if you are willing to give me the money because you thought I looked good, then I'm going to take it. That's it.

A lot of women have love for you but you have no love for them. That's a Catch 22 situation. They love you, and that's the reason why they give you money. If you've got two or three women like this, I don't mind if they spend all their money on me, put it all in my hand.

It was all about the money to me, nothing else. I'd be making about $800 to $1,000 a week off these women, a shitload more than I was getting breaking my back at the loading dock.

I didn't think about what this was doing to my soul, the price that was being paid to get this money. What I was doing was not what a man should stand for. Eventually, I would realize that all of this stuff was coming to a head. It was coming to a close, and something had to change.

Before it did, though, I wasn't going to tell Evon shit about what I was doing. It ain't her business, that was my attitude. So long as I am taking care of business, paying the bills, putting food on the table, that's all that mattered. Some of the women I'd be hustling would be right in Evon's face, and she never knew. We were in Vegas for about eight months when I reckon Evon started asking herself what's going on. She must have asked herself, "He's not hanging out with me so he must be doing something not right and obviously it has to do with another woman." When you're coming home with woman's smells and all kind of shit on your clothes, women pick up on this real quick. With me, I did not give a fuck. I don't care what you think and what you feel, okay?

While Evon had suspicions about me, the thing that really blew our relationship apart was something she had done before we had got together. I found out that she'd had a lesbian affair and, when I came to think about it, I think she may have been lesbian all the time. It disturbed me so much that, every time I looked at her, it wasn't the lesbian affair which disgusted me, it was the lies and the secrets. How dare you marry me knowing that this is who you are, okay? How dare you?

At that point in time, it was on, the violence was on, the ass whipping. I couldn't stand to see her face. She made me sick 'cos I loved her, but I would never trust her again. It was something that I couldn't accept at all. She should have told me. I wasn't thinking about what I was doing, screwing around, hustling, and how that had looked to her, what was right or wrong. I was only thinking what was right for Alex.

We stayed together for another five or six months and in that time we never had a rational conversation about it as it just made me angry and more abusive. I couldn't stand her, but I didn't not want to be married either. See, I'm still trying to make something happen. I don't know how to accept this thing. I felt like it was something that had happened to me, but it hadn't – it was something that had happened to her.

I decided, from that moment on, that anyone coming into my life was going to get shit off me. I closed up, all the way. Everything became work to me. Every woman I came across was work, hustling. Love, I ain't going to love none of you bitches, period. Matter of fact I am going to hate you. You disgust me.

Evon was selling real estate or something and eventually moved out into her own place, which left me free to hustle even more. One thing about women when they see you've got your own shit, they gravitate towards you. They see you in your own place, your own car, no other woman around. There were other motherfuckers out there hustling like me, but they were all flash but I was different, young and all clean cut. I'd have three or four women I'd be playing at the one time, giving me the money, believing everything I said but it was all a lie.

In Vegas, of course, I was still chasing the music. I was singing with a group called The Monarchs. It was Kal Howard and the boys. They were a good band, but over time I discovered Vegas was not the place to go to try and collect stardom. Being a lounge act in Vegas then, and it's the same now, is not going to get you a record deal. I quickly realized as a black act in Vegas they weren't going to let you go any further than singing 50 versions of the songs the white folks and tourists wanted to hear such as "Ain't No Stopping Us Now" by McFadden & Whitehead, "Reunited" by Peaches & Herb, all that kind of shit.

After about a year in Vegas, I called this girl I knew who worked in Minneapolis, Barbara Kelly, and told her I needed to get back there and could she send me a ticket. I'd known Barbara from before and, even though she was five or six years older than me and she had a daughter, I really liked her. When I went back to Minneapolis all my shit was in a brown paper bag, I felt lower than a dog but I was determined to put to use what I'd learned from my time in Jackson and Vegas.

I moved in with Barbara and everything was cool when after about eight months she told me she was pregnant and wanted an abortion. As soon as she told me that, I slapped the shit out of her. I had no kids but wanted a child, and now she wanted to get rid of it. I think the reason she wanted an abortion was that, when we'd got together, she'd just come out of a relationship. I think she might have still been seeing this guy and slept with him and didn't know who the fuck the father was. That could have been the reason. Another reason could be I was too immature to be a father, which I was. Barbara knew what she needed for a father and she knew I wasn't going to be there, so she threw me out.

Thank you Barbara Kelly though for teaching me a valuable lesson – I decided I would never again live with a woman without having my own place. A woman will never again be able to kick Alexander O'Neal out on to the street.

At this moment in time, from all my experiences, I was almost like a woman hater. I wouldn't give any woman the time of day. I simply didn't trust them at all. A woman could say something, swear to God that she'll never do this or that – then the next minute she's turned the whole world upside-down. I didn't trust women but I needed them for my hustling – and, for hustling, I had to look good.

Every day I'd be playing two hours of basketball then back to the apartment and doing sit ups and shit. I was 176 pounds – that's 12st 8lb – and I'd realized that the better I look, the finer I am and the more bitches are going to want to be with me. When they see this new fine black man in town, they gotta have some of that. What they don't know is what lies behind that – my whole philosophy is I'm not going to be with a woman if she's not going to pay. I won't have nothing to do with her. Simple.

I knew what the total package was and, at the time, I felt that was me.

When my music became more successful, I went to a different level of hustling. All the cats who thought they were the pretty boys and think they're this that and the other, they can't fuck with you. Number One: you'll kick their fucking ass. Number Two: you are better looking than them and Number Three: you are talented. With those three combinations that's a recipe for money, in Minneapolis, that's a recipe for fast, hardcore money. It was path I followed – along with building my music career – for the next six or seven years.

In this period there were some women who were the exception rather than the rule.

One was a hooker everyone in town knew, Roxanne Chuson. I loved her and I didn't give a shit who knew it and that we were together. If she earned her living as a hooker that was her business, not mine. When she was with me, she was my woman, and that's all that mattered to me. We weren't destined to be together for life, but it was never going to be some remarkable story where she changed her life and I changed my life and we went on to be Mr and Mrs. That wasn't on the cards. Maybe if we had kids it could have been different.

Roxanne liked her drink, her beer. She would get drunk and start running off her mouth. She'd get brassy, and I'd slap her around.

Another girl I had a relationship was Michelle, who I met in a Downtown club called Moby Dicks. I'd been invited up on stage to sing with a band called the TC Jammers, and my now very good friend Bobby Vandell was their drummer. I remember I did Bobby Caldwell's "What You Won't Do For Love". Nights like this I'd come off stage and then walk round the club checking out all the chicks, knowing you are going to get chosen by one of them. Michelle and her girlfriend were sitting there and they both liked me, but Michelle was the one who made a move. Me, I'm always open to my next move.

Michelle had it going on. She was the manager at a restaurant, had her own place, her own car. It was right up my alley, and we got together.

Michelle is the one responsible for me being here today. Imagine that, a woman responsible for Alexander O'Neal? What Michelle did was recognize my talent and decide, "I am going to make sure you don't want for anything, need anything so you can just concentrate on your music." And that's what happened. I still hustled but I didn't need to hustle. She was taking care of me. Everything that I needed was in Michelle but, over time, this relationship also ran its course.

Many years later, I was in a relationship with Natasha – more of her later – but I maintained a relationship with Michelle. By this time my life had changed, but then Michelle hit me with the big surprise – she was pregnant. I said, "I thought you couldn't get pregnant?" Now I was in a situation where she had tied us together for the rest of our lives. I didn't resent it, I accepted it and tried to make the best of it. Then along comes my daughter, Catrice, and I am determined to have a relationship with her. I had given her my name because she was my girl, my daughter and I loved her.

I guess I wasn't happy or unhappy – I just took it as the game. I didn't plan on spending my life with these people. We had Catrice and I love her. I never regretted any of my kids, even though they didn't know the circumstances in which they came into this world. I am being honest. When you are young, you think everything is cute and fun until the woman you are not even in love with tells you she is going to have your baby. What do you do? You don't do stupid things. You got yourself into it and it takes two to tango. I accepted the fact that this is what I had got myself into so I had to deal with it. I never had to pay child support or anything like that because I always tried to be the kind of father who took care of my kids. I have always told their mothers if they need me I am there. They don't have to put the system on me.

Michelle and I continued on after the baby was born. I was still very fond of her until it came to a point where my behaviour was too overbearing. I've got the deal now and the women thing has escalated, it really has. Women coming out of the damn woodwork, everything. First, they get adjusted to the fact that you are a recording artist and now you are a "star". As soon as that comes into play then, all of a sudden, chicks that you see in clubs who never talk to you are all up on you. Chicks are trying to seek you out.

There was one girl, Sharon Olbekson, who was just someone I was seeing late at night. I'd call her after the club and then go round. I never took her out or anything. We didn't have a relationship as such but she ended up getting pregnant with twins, my daughters Louisa and Siana.

See, all these women – they all loved me more than I loved them. I don't mean I didn't have any love at all for them, just that they loved me way more. That's how they became vulnerable.

My own behaviour, the hustling, had also extracted a price. What happens is that you lose some of yourself when you sell yourself like that. That's a thing I would never accept, selling my whole life away like that.

I knew in my heart that I had to change and make a life for myself.

CHAPTER 4

Minneapolis

The Twin Cities is a very Scandinavian-orientated area. Back in the early 1970s, there was a mass of TV and radio stations there, but black people couldn't be a part of it.

Coming out of Chicago there was a wealth of black radio stations and down south in Mississippi it was the same. In Natchez, you could pick stations up out of Memphis and New Orleans. The stations would all be owned by old traditional white people but they always knew the importance of black music. When I went to Minneapolis, it was a totally different story and that was a culture shock to me. There was only one little radio station called KUXL that played R&B music. It was a hell of a struggle. I was frustrated. We were bouncing around with our music but didn't have anywhere to take it.

We performed in black pubs, but they weren't clubs. There were only two black clubs that I knew of which was Nacirema on the south side and the VFW but you could only play at these places at the weekend. At the Nacirema we would play Friday, Saturday and Sunday night. The band I was in at this time was called Enterprise Band of Pleasure, which was owned by a guy called Mahreedy Holmes and Morris Day was on drums.

As close as we were, Mahreedy and I used to fight like cats and dogs. Mahreedy grew up hard in Michael Jackson's home town, Gary, Indiana. He would always be trying to show me that he was hard and, at the end of the day, he thought he could whoop my ass. He might have thought that but it would never happen 'cos I knew I could take care of business. We were always threatening, be in each other's face, we would be one click away from throwing a blow. I would be standing there waiting with a, "What you gonna do?" type of attitude. But we didn't dislike each other enough to be throwing blows. He might have disliked the way I was, it could have been arrogance, I don't know. It's like Terry Lewis always says about me, "Alex O'Neal is a great guy but if he doesn't have respect for you, he'll walk over you like a doormat."

No matter how much we fought, Mahreedy helped me out tremendously. He helped me to develop my talent and bring it to the forefront. He taught me how to play things on the piano, and he was an excellent keyboard player. He taught me how to strengthen my voice, sing from the diaphragm. He taught me things I didn't know and for that, I will be eternally grateful. We both wanted success in music. I ended up recording a whole bunch of songs with him.

This whole phase of my career was learning my craft.

Prince used to come out to our shows on Sunday night, not often but every now and then. You'd get the message just before we'd go out to perform, "Prince is in the house, he's in the corner, hiding."

Him and Morris had been friends a long time.

With things going slow in Minneapolis, me and Mahreedy set out to Los Angeles to try and land a record deal. We recorded these songs, printed up our bios and headed out West. For the journey to LA, I am driving a brand new 1980 Chrysler Diplomat. We drove from Minneapolis to East Moline, Illinois where we picked up Nate Lawrence who was Mahreedy's manager. We hit Highway 80 and proceeded to head off for LA to drop off our tapes at record companies and see if we got any response. We never got there.

We were sharing the driving, but I was dog tired from the night before and fell asleep at the wheel 25 miles from Des Moines, Iowa. I woke up when the car hit the guardrail. I snatched the wheel but that just flipped the car and the next minute it was spinning and flipped over like some shit you see on TV or a movie. I knew I wasn't going to die – I just knew it.

Here we are upside down rolling across one of the biggest highways in the country and all I am thinking are the other guys okay? "Mahreedy, Nate, y'all all right? Y'all right, man?"

That's all I could say. The car skidded right across both sides of the highway before ending up in a ditch upside down, the wheels still spinning.

Incredibly we got out of the car just with just scratches. The car, brand new, was totalled. Man, you couldn't believe how we got out of that car alive. I went back in the car after I helped get the other guys out. What did I go in for, the tapes? No, an ounce of weed.

A guy named Clarence Jackson from Des Moines, a friend of Nate, was a Godsend. Clarence picked me, pepped me up and let me know that shit happens and just take strength from the fact we were all alive. I was traumatized from that event and it has left a lasting scar. Even today I won't let anybody drive me until I am sure I can trust them with my life.

We weren't deterred by the crash – someone drove us back to O'Hare airport in Chicago and we got a plane to Los Angeles.

We didn't know what the process was for getting a record. We didn't know anyone in LA who we could ask for help or bring our stuff to. We were going around blind, hoping we'd just walk in somewhere and someone would say our stuff is really good. It was good stuff but looking back today I think the material we had was not commercial enough. I think one of the issues we had was Mahreedy instead of being a hardcore R&B player, was more of a jazz and blues player. It was probably the wrong sound for that time. Mahreedy was still with a sound that had come and gone. Nate tried four or five record companies but struck out – nobody was interested.

It was time to go back to Minneapolis, but first I went to Las Vegas to pick up my car from Evon. Even though I'd just been in a major car wreck, I drove it myself, two days, back to the Twin Cities. Every time I thought I was getting tired, I pulled the fuck over.

I had no time to be disappointed about how things had panned out in LA. I had come that close to death, it was right up in my face. Most motherfuckers who have a wreck like this do not come out of it. They are either paralyzed or dead. I was on a high from being alive – I ain't got time to be disappointed.

Back in Minneapolis, I carried on playing with Enterprise for a while when a band called Flyte Tyme came calling. They were the biggest black band in the city.

The group was made up of Cynthia Johnson, lead vocals and sax; Terry Lewis on bass guitar; Jimmy Jam Harris on keyboard; Monte Moir on keyboard; Solomon Hughes and Gary Jellybean Johnson on drums.

Terry Lewis was a very efficient guy, very organized. He used to haul the equipment around with his brother, Jerome, and two other guys, Popeye and a guy called Prince (not that one!). We'd come over to help but most of the time he'd always have it done, that was his thing.

Now at the time the band was always used to having a woman as lead singer, they weren't used to a man up front but I think I was the best available, man or woman. Cynthia Johnson had just quit the band and gone off with a guy called Steve Greenberg to form the group Lipps, Inc. (a pun on the phrase "lip-synch"). Great move for her, as it turned out, 'cos the band had a smash hit the world over with the song "Funkytown". When it happened for her, I was so pleased for Cynthia because she really is a great person, a lovely sweet girl.

When I took her place in Flyte Tyme, I could tell they didn't really want me as part of the band, they liked my voice but only wanted me to be a frontman, like the Wynd Chymes had back in Jackson.

For me, I knew this was a great opportunity to really move my career along. Flyte Tyme were the resident band at the Riverview Supper Club where we performed every Thursday, Friday and Saturday night, me opening the show normally with something from the likes of Teddy Pendergrass. Whether they liked it or not, over time I became a hardcore part of the band.

I was a few years older than most of the group and they knew I was a different kind of bird to them. Back then I was just starting out with snorting cocaine, always smoked weed, all day, every day. None of the rest of the band drank, smoked or did anything. My behaviour must have annoyed the shit out of them, but I was a bold bird. They used to tease me, and Terry Lewis would mimic how I spoke and acted on weed or coke but it was no big deal. This was the late 1970s, early 1980s.

We became really popular and a couple of times, when big bands were visiting the city and performing at the 2,600-capacity Orpheum Theater, Flyte Tyme were asked to open. I remember we did this for gigs by bands like The Bar-Kays and Cameo. For a Minneapolis audience to see a local band playing such a big venue was something new. We were making waves. In fact with ourselves, Prince and the singer Rockie Robbins, who'd been signed to A&M Records, Minneapolis was starting to get on the R&B map. The success we were having led to the opening of a new black radio station, KMOJ, which could reach the south side of the city and our music spread.

Gradually it started to dawn on me that I was at home on the big stage and if I was good enough to open shows for these big groups then one day why can't some motherfuckers open shows for me? I knew I was good enough one day to be a star.

I was crossing all my "Ts" and dotting all my "I's". I was beginning to really understand that I had something, the difference between talent and a gift. We had a lot of great singers and musicians in Minneapolis but I asked myself: "Why do I stand out?"

CHAPTER 5
Fatherhood

While I was playing with Flyte Tyme at the Riverview Supper Club, I was to meet Natasha Diamond, the woman who would later become the mother of the first two of my nine children. She was a hairdresser at the time and came up to me and started talking to me about doing my hair. She gave me her card and a few days later I gave her a call to make an 'appointment'. We ended up being together for probably three years and had two kids.

Tasha had more experience with people than me. She was married before and had a son, but her husband got killed. He got stabbed in Compton and bled to death. This guy was a hustler to say the least and a very good-looking man, but he had a lot of women.

Like a lot of my relationships, it was very much an on/off affair. We would be together and then break up, be together, break up. I knew in my head that we were not destined to stay together, but then one day she broke the news to me that she was pregnant with my first child, Carlton. The fact she was pregnant was a bit of a shock. I mean, hell, for 28 years I thought I'd been shooting blanks. Everybody else was having all these kids, but for me, with all these women, nothing was happening. There was the time when I was with Barbara when she said she was pregnant, but I didn't know if the kid was mine. Since then, all the other women I had been with, nothing.

Man, I always wanted kids, even when I was 14 years old. I wanted to be one of them young fathers who made a mistake and had kids. I would have loved that situation. Tasha already had a kid from her previous marriage, a five-year-old son called Alfred.

As I said, when I lived with Tasha, we'd have our highs and lows as usual, and I'd move out again. I was "out" when she had the baby.

I didn't even know he was born until a friend of hers asked me, "Have you been to see your son?" and I went like, "I didn't know she had the baby."

When my son came along, then we tried to be together again, but I didn't have any concept at 28 years old. I had no concept of family. I was definitely a "papa was a rolling stone" kinda guy. Tasha, I think she might have been looking for something a little more permanent, but I wasn't willing to not only give it to her but to give it to anybody at that point.

Even with Carlton coming along, I was always a hustler, and Tasha knew it. At that point in time, I didn't really have any respect for women, not to care about their needs. And, certainly, I didn't know anything about being a family man. That I knew nothing about.

All I knew was how to play a role to get what I wanted. I was in a different place.

When I was with Tasha – and other women I lived with – I always had my own place to fall back to. I always had a key to turn that was mine, whether it was a small room or a rented apartment. I was determined that I would never get kicked out. I'm not going to put myself in that kind of position to be living under a woman's roof where she can kick me out. If she thinks that she can kick me out, then go ahead and do it, I'll be fine. That was the lesson I learned when Barbara had kicked me out.

Tasha had Alfred and Carlton, but the way I was living she knew she didn't have me. She had a lot of problems with that.

I was 28 years old, dawg. I'm singing in the clubs. I'm finding out that I'm not just good, I have been given a gift and this is my destiny. I've also realized that women find me attractive and I got attention from all kinds of girls. I've slept with all kinds of women – I was 28 and sleeping with women aged 55, okay? Anything that came into my path, woman-wise, at that point in time in my life, was fair game. It was about game, okay?

Tasha knew about my behaviour but we both still tried to make it work even though we were such volatile people. We both possessed some of the same type of craziness when angry. Even though I had feelings for Tasha – maybe one could call it love, maybe not – but they weren't enough to make me want to stay with her, okay?

I wasn't the kind of guy who suited marriage. I wasn't the man with two kids, trying hard to be married, trying to keep the family together. I was still into, "This is my son. You're the mother of my kid. That's what it is and nothing more." Now at that point in time, I didn't know what the hell we both were bargaining and buying, because when you have a kid out of wedlock – especially with Tasha – all hell breaks loose, okay? I don't think that she was ever using Carlton, the baby, to attack me – she's not that kind of woman. She don't give a shit about none of that.

Tasha is a very independent woman. She was independent when I met her. She'd been on her own for a long time, even before she was an adult. We do that in Minneapolis. Women, young women, they would be on their own at 17 and 18 years old. They would be in an apartment. They have their own motherfucking place, man.

With Carlton, we both fought like cats and dogs. I fought to stay in my son's life. I think she fought just because I was there. That was enough reason, just because I was there. I don't think she had any malice towards me, I don't think it was that kind of thing, I don't think that she hated me. We would fight because, at that time, I was ignorant of how I should behave. If I didn't know how to treat a wife, how the fuck would I know how to treat a woman who's had my baby? How would I know that? I didn't and I kept behaving like a single man and I would dare her or anybody else to question it. If you don't like it, I can step away. She was in her own place, but I can step, because I always got places to go. That wasn't really what she wanted, I don't think, but soon she started to realize that there was no fairytale ending here. This is not going to be that kind of relationship.

Eventually, of course, we broke up but the fighting between us didn't stop. When she put up her dukes and started fighting, she made my life a fucking homie hell for about five years. Definitely the more success I got, the more away from her I grew, the angrier she'd be.

I'd walked away from her but I was determined that I would never give up with my son. I would never, in a billion years, give him up. Tasha accepted that he would still be in my life and he spent a lot of time with me as a baby, little boy stuff, and I thank her for that. For her, it must have been hard because she knew I had these other women in my life and obviously if Carlton's going to be with me, he's going to be around them.

She knew some of the women and she couldn't stand them. She hated Michelle, and I can tell you that right now. Michelle was a real go-getter and had given me a daughter in Catrice so Tasha thought she was probably taking very good care of me. I suppose I flaunted my relationship with her in Tasha's face. There was one time I drove Michelle's car to Tasha's house. What did Tasha do? She slashed all the goddamn tyres.

Driving Michelle's car was me showing I didn't give a shit – I'm not staying, I'm not with you. It didn't matter to Tasha – she was crazy like that.

I suppose it didn't help that every so often we'd still go to bed together. We'd be out late night on a Sunday. I'd go see my son, and I'd hit it. I'd be having sex with Tasha.

It took time 'til it dawned on me that the only way that Tasha and I were ever going to have a chance of having a friendship and winning each other's respect is to stop having sex. Because every time you have sex those feelings resurface. Her feelings are resurfacing and constantly rekindling the fire.

Nothing would get better until we both let go, until she was seeing other people and had her own friends and I could do whatever I wanted.

Some of the things that came out of Tasha's mouth would be enough for me to know that I'm never going to be with her because I can't stand women who are like that. I can't stand women who say nasty, crazy things. Everything always had to go to the nasty level with her. We'd be arguing on the phone, some shit would come out of her mouth and it'd seem like I'm never going to see my son again. Every day saying, "So long as I have a hold of this boy."

This ain't just one or two times – this was three or four times a day. I'd be with Michelle and Tasha would be calling and hanging up, calling and hanging up, all hours of the night, all hours of the day.

She was in control of that part of my life and now I was beginning to resent her. I was beginning to resent any woman who knows that she cannot be with a man and yet still talks to that man like she's with him. Have a fight with him like she's with him. Have a bad day and he comes to pick his son up, and all hell breaks loose.

Most of this was on the phone. There was a lot of swearing back and forth, hard swearing, that's what I call nasty. That was not the answer to the question for her or for me, that type of behaviour, but we were in our twenties. She's thinking, "He's younger than me, so what the hell does he think he's going to get?"

Tasha was like a pitbull – they're wonderful with people, but not with another dog. A pitbull don't give a fuck about another dog.

If it's another woman, Tasha kept the same distance from all of them. There ain't no, "I hate you", "I like you." She ain't like none of them. She don't fuck with them, and them bitches better not come up in her face about nothing. She ain't trying to be nice, ain't trying to be friends. "I don't like you, fuck you", that's the name of that tune.

That was kind of difficult later on to deal with when you have a kid, and the kid is at your house with your wife and your two daughters.

Tasha, she's a good woman, I ain't going to say she's not. She'd do damn near anything to keep me happy. But you've got to want to be happy with a woman before you can allow her to make you happy.

Happiness was not something that I gave a fuck about. I make myself happy. I'm my best friend, and that was my policy. I don't need no motherfucker to make me happy, and I don't need an excuse as to why today I'm feeling this way or that. She was a very good woman in that respect, but when she made me happy, then I'd turn around and make her sad and hurt her. She'd get hurt by my behaviour. At that point, either she'd leave or I'd leave.

Looking back on the time we were together, look what we got from it. We got to be saddled with each other for the rest our lives. Because, when you have a child together, it should be for life. To some people, a child may not be as important to them as it was to me. I doted on that boy. Me and him, from when he was a baby, from an infant all the way up, we hung out. It was Alex, his car seat and his son.

With Tasha and me, things didn't get better in our relationship until we just started growing as adults, talking and respecting each other. I don't know if she ever respected me at that time. I know she does now, and we respect each other.

We stopped the bullshit and that was good for both of us. Then we kind of grew up at that point in time because we were two young people with a baby. I was never going to give my son up. I was not going to be one of the fathers that would walk away. I was going to be in his life, hard. The boy meant so much to me then and still does today. I was saying to Tasha, whether I'm with you or not with you, I have put up with everything that you have thrown at me. But I am not going to walk away from Carlton because of you. You might as well get ready for that 'cos we've got a long fight ahead. I didn't know when that shit was going to be over. I thought, I didn't have experience with raising no kid, stuff like that, but I was always a good man, a kind person and a giving person.

After we broke up for good, Tasha didn't chase me for a quarter, she never asked me for shit. She never asked me for a dime, she isn't that kind of a woman. I'm the kind of man you don't have to ask for anything. If she had asked me for something, I would have surely given it to her, but she didn't. The more she didn't ask me for something, the more she felt we wouldn't be tied.

I would have done anything for Tasha had she asked me, but she was too proud to ask. She didn't give a damn if the whole fucking building was burning down around her. She wouldn't ask me for shit. I had a relationship with her other son, Al, and – when stardom came – I realized that I couldn't treat Carlton one way and treat Al another. I loved them both to death.

She was very gracious and she trusted me. Al and Carlton would come to my house and I also took them out on the road and showed them some things. When I had them out on the road, I'm like, "Everybody around me, look. If anything happens with these boys, you motherfuckers might as well just be gone off the face of the earth. I swear to God. I'm trusting you. I'm in New York City. You know I got interviews. You know I got shit to do. I'm trusting you. You just make sure nothing happens to these boys, okay?"

Together Tasha and I built our own relationship with the boys.

It's a relationship that we've sustained until this day, and I admire her for it. Al's definitely in my heart. I love him to death.

Tasha and I still had our ups and downs, especially when she hooked up with this other guy, a doctor. He moved her and the boys, when Carlton was about seven, to New York.

All I give a fuck about is Al and Carlton and this doctor took my son to New York City, goddamn it. I tell you that shit drove me crazy. Knowing that he's going to go from Minneapolis to hardcore New York City. I was livid but there was nothing I could do. Tasha, she was waiting, she was just thinking, "I dare you to say something." But I couldn't say anything. I couldn't say, "I'm going to take the boy." I could do nothing.

I know New York, and I know how kids there work. They're like grown ups. These little kids got their own codes to the street. I mean, he was getting threatened just because he was an outsider. Motherfucker, in the Minneapolis school system they don't get threatened because they're outsiders. You get threatened because you got into some shit with a motherfucker, right? In New York, you get threatened because you're a punk ass motherfucker and they'll kick, stab you up, shoot, all kinds of shit. And Carlton was having those kinds of problems.

Goddamn, if something really bad had happened to that boy, man, you would have seen all about it. I don't have enough money. I don't have enough money to exhaust to take you to the depths of hell.

I think that was one of the only things that prompted her to move back to Minneapolis and bring him back. She knew something had happened to that boy.

When she came back, Tasha and I finally found a place in the middle where we could deal with each other. I think she realized that she needed me because she needed a father who cared about his child.

She didn't need Alexander O'Neal for shit herself. But she needed a father that cared about his child.

Back in Minneapolis, Carlton started giving her hell. He'd call it back and forth. I mean this kid, wow. The more we gave him, the more he seemed to gravitate to some negative shit, some bullshit. Tasha did her best, and I did as well as I could. But would it all add up to being a conventional family? Hell no.

I'd take Carlton to my house and I had to force him to do his school work. If I hadn't, he wouldn't even have graduated high school. "You're not going to deny yourself this," I'd say to him. "High school by itself don't mean a goddamn thing except for anyone that sees you as a potential, that at an early age you have the ability to complete something. That's all it means. Back in my days, if you're in high school, you get a good education, you get a good job."

So, between Tasha and me, between her household and my household, we dragged him through. She didn't go through as much as I did because she couldn't handle it, his crazy behaviour.

All I wanted from Carlton is for him to have everything he ever wanted and needed. It's all I want, and it covers everything I didn't have as a kid.

CHAPTER 6
Prince and me

Three years after his first album, Prince was one of the biggest stars on the planet and could call the tune with his record company. One of the things he wanted, alongside his own career, was to create a new group which he'd manage and produce himself. He was helped by his friend Morris Day, who'd been in a high school band with him.

Morris and I had got to know each other on the Minneapolis scene and together we'd been offered an audition to join a group out of Illinois that were called Champaign, who had a big hit with a track called "How 'Bout Us". We'd done the audition and Morris was offered the gig as a drummer, but they turned me down. I didn't get the gig because, although the record company loved my voice, they wanted to stick with Pauli Carman who'd sung lead vocals on their hit record. Turned out they had their problems with Pauli, who was one of those uncontrollable brothers. The band wanted to kick Pauli out, but the record company pulled the strings. In the end Morris turned the gig down 'cos he had an "in" with Prince back in Minneapolis, which is where he thought he could get a better deal. That's exactly how it turned out.

Prince had grown up in Minneapolis and had played many of the same clubs as we had before he'd broken into the big time with his first album, *For You*, in 1978. In fact, the producer who had worked with Prince to get him his first break was Chris Moon, with whom I'd also been doing some recording work.

Make no mistake, I think Prince was an absolute genius, but

I honestly believe that the music he created was born out of the "Minneapolis Sound" that myself and other musicians in the city were creating. All of us played on a different level, but the sound that Prince brought to the world was one that was definitely spawned by a lot of people. Prince didn't come up with the sound himself. He developed it.

In the time I was building my career it was crucial to me to remain true to my roots and develop my R&B sound. I never wanted to achieve success by watering down what I was doing just so I could be played on white radio stations. No thanks.

That wasn't the choice Prince made. He was from the same black community as me, but it didn't run as deep.

Prince was black when it was convenient for him to be black. It wasn't something that he gravitated towards – he gravitated to his white genes, his white side, his mother's side. He was a very light-skinned brother, and it was a long time before Prince even dealt with black people, a long time before he came into himself. Prince, to me, didn't preach who he was. He didn't think he was white but his whole world, well that was the Caucasian world.

It was a long time before Prince even dealt with black people. For a long time, they were a no-no for him. He is gone now, and the Lord bless his soul, but being black wasn't good enough for Prince.

By the time of his third album *Dirty Mind* he only had two black cats in his touring band and he had them looking white. André Cymone, his bass player, was the exception. He was still black and still conducted himself like that, and he still had black friends.

That was time when black people couldn't even come around Prince. You wouldn't be around Prince, no way. To me, some light must have gone off in Prince's head where he said to himself, "Wait a minute, I can't do this". From that point on, he decided not to recognize his own blackness. Years later, all of a sudden, he turns the whole thing around and it's all black. Suddenly you've got all these people in his band and they're all black – you know, loud suits, funny hats and shit like that – and they play their asses off.

Why weren't they good enough to play with you when you were doing all the white shit? Why weren't they good enough, man? Why did you surround your whole self with white people? Why? Why was that necessary? When you came out, guess what you were wearing? You wore the biggest afro in the States.

You can have greatness and you don't have to compromise who you are. You don't have to be anything but who you are. If anybody don't get it, then they can just go to hell. People like Jimi Hendrix knew that. He was a black man and he acted like that, like an intelligent black man. Lenny Kravitz is a monster player, and a monster star, but I don't think he ever stopped being black.

I thought Prince treated us black people like shit for quite a while.

Let's just call a spade a spade. Prince thought we weren't as good as white people. We weren't good enough to be around in his entourage, that's for damn sure. All those great musicians he could have chosen, but he'd be going over to the other side of town to pick some white boy.

The press told me that, when he fired me, Prince said I was too black. I guess I am too black, but I'm never going to compromise how proud I am of who I am and where I'm from. That's going to be first with me and foremost in anything that I do.

I was raised in Mississippi and don't have time to sit there judging nobody, telling them how to think and how to feel. I just react on how you react towards me. What I have seen with Prince, one of the biggest stars ever, was he didn't have respect for black people for a long time.

Now, I know that many black friends and public figures may

argue with me on this issue. That's because "you" wasn't there. You weren't in Minneapolis, you weren't a musician right along with a guy who was there.

Before Prince had a deal, he didn't have a pot to piss in or a window to throw it out of. He was living with André and the Anderson family in north Minneapolis.

Once he got a deal, I don't know if he was kind to them. I would want to hope that he was very kind to them. I don't believe it, but I would hope it.

These memories make me angry. They make me bitter. And, to me, it will always be part of Prince's legacy. I don't know if that tarnishes his legacy in anybody's mind and I hope it doesn't, because that's not what I'm talking about here. I'm not talking about his accomplishments, his achievements. I'm talking about the man. A lot of people didn't know the man. I only knew what the man showed me.

I had a lot of this shit in my mind when one morning I got a call from Morris asking if I could come and see him and Prince and when I turned up they outlined what they wanted. Morris was to be the drummer in a new band managed by Prince and I was to be the lead singer. The band would tour with Prince, opening his shows, all stuff like that. It was going to be controlled by Prince, but we didn't know it was going to be controlled by Prince, for Prince, with Prince. Prince was into this rock 'n' roll stuff, and the new band was going to be like The BusBoys, black rock 'n' roll.

Prince and Morris come to my house the next night and picked me up and we went to Rudolph's restaurant. Prince started laying out this thing about the band, he wanted me and Flyte Tyme. Everything was fine, but I wasn't all that excited as a motherfucker should be, sitting there with Prince, 'cos I had never liked Prince. At the time, I felt that I'd kick his little punk ass.

I'd already had a bad encounter with Prince on some shit years before at a show. That time I was in a group called the Black Market Band and we were doing a New Year's Eve gig. Prince was performing with his band, Champagne, not to be confused with the one that me and Morris had tried out for.

We were down as the headline act but we didn't know anything about being headliners. Prince had a little more knowledge about this stuff and, after another group had opened the show, he came on just before we were due to play.

That little motherfucker played all over our set. When we got onstage, it was seven minutes before midnight and they were getting ready to shut the damn hotel down. He did that deliberately.

I'll never ever forget that. There he was with his musicians, laughing and joking on stage, and Morris Day was the drummer. All of them in that band were light-skinned, every one of them. What is that telling you? What the fuck is that telling you? I saw it in Prince's face, I saw it in his eyes. Him and his band were fucking us over through music. Laughing and joking and playing. They weren't getting off until they got tired. They played like they were ending the show. Now, some people do things like that. I would never do any shit like that. I wouldn't do that, not to another peer, I wouldn't do that.

Your time is your time. You go on, you got your time, you go and you play. But not Prince.

That let me know what kind of person he was right then and there. I don't care if he is young or not but anybody that would do that kind of shit is a selfish, self-centered motherfucker.

Half the audience was there to see us, the. Prince didn't give a shit and none of them gave a shit. After that, for a long time, Prince would be one of those guys that I wouldn't have anything to do with because I called him two-faced and that would have got back to him.

Now here he was trying to offer me a job.

I suppose many people would have bitten their hand off at the opportunity they were offering me, but I've always been an independent, strong-willed type of guy. I certainly wasn't no ass kisser.

We started recording two or three songs at Prince's house when I started asking questions.

I guess my mouth did not allow me to accept the opportunity they were presenting. The problem was that I wanted to know how everything was going to be handled and how the deal would work. And it seems they didn't like it.

I was also asking about Jellybean Johnson, Flyte Tyme's drummer. I said, if you are going to take Flyte Tyme, the whole band, what's going to happen to Jellybean if Morris is going to be the new band's drummer? That didn't seem right to me. It wasn't right for someone who had put all that time into the band to be left walking down the street with nothing.

The question I asked could have been answered, and it didn't have to be perceived as a threat, as someone who is uncontrollable.

Prince and Morris instead looked at each other like: what kind of question is that? What's going to happen to Jellybean? Why are you concerned with that? You should only be concerned with yourself.

Morris hadn't asked any questions. He knows the answer to the question, and that's to kiss Prince's ass until you get your deal. If Prince wants you to pick someone up from the airport, you go do it, whatever he wants you do it. I ain't mad at Morris for doing that, it was his opportunity and I am not upset at him for having done that. But it's just not who I am. I cannot be part of that, and I am not going to kiss ass.

They shouldn't have been intimidated by me asking business

questions and being inquisitive about certain things. I understand that, when you are in the formative stage of your career, as Prince was then, sometimes certain people have a need to control everyone and everything around them. Alexander O'Neal doesn't live on those kind of terms. You can't control me, nobody can control me. There is nothing that would make me give up control of myself and bow down to you. You're younger than me and you think I'm going to bow down to you because you're Prince? It ain't happening, dog.

While all this stuff was going on, Flyte Tyme had gigs still to do. So I'm wondering why we are not rehearsing? Turns out these motherfuckers had already been rehearsing with Prince, but nobody told me. It was a hush-hush thing, "Don't say shit to Alex about this, we'll handle it."

They were saying, fuck Alex. We'll take this band, which is excellent, and we'll put Morris as the lead singer. We'll keep Jellybean, the guy he was asking about, and instead we'll get rid of his ass. And that's what they did. It was ugly and nasty the way they did it. No one told me or was man enough to say that they had signed the deal with Prince. These were all my boys, people I thought were friends. But obviously they weren't.

I honestly thought we didn't need Prince. I kept trying to talk to Terry and say, "Look man, keep writing the stuff, man, and we are going to get our own deal." Here I am, being all gullible and naïve, talking about our accomplishments, all this shit.

But the band had decided no. Going with Prince was a quicker and better way. I had been stabbed in the back in every way that you could be.

We were doing what became our last gig, I had cracked my wrist and was in excruciating pain with a cast on my wrist. These guys were so cruel I am singing a song and the parts I am singing are not the ones they're singing. They'd taken another part out of a song called "Cool" with the lines "I am cool 'til I'm dead." They'd signed the deal, and they were grinning at each other. They knew something I didn't know. Eventually Terry Lewis was the one who told me what was going down. I was out, and they were in.

To fans in Minneapolis, Flyte Tyme was always known as The Tyme. Prince simply swapped the "y" for an "i" and The Time was formed. It was to become one of the hottest bands in the country.

Was it painful? Yes. Was it humiliating? Fuck yes.

I got kicked out because I asked one fucking question – what's going to happen to Jellybean? Him and Terry were the mainstays of the band.

Stupid me, stupid question. But I've got a big fucking heart, and I need to know these things. Is this person going to get fucked over by you just so the band can get a deal with you?

Next thing I began to read and hear I was out of the band 'cos I was "too black". Too black in my pigmentation, or too black because I am too opinionated? That I look like a black man and stand up, do my whole thing like a black man? You've been around these white folks. You're half white – your whole perception of blackness is not the same as mine. Your journey is one where you haven't seen anything in your life. I am talking about Prince and Morris, all those "high yella" light-skinned boys.

I was out. I was hurt and felt betrayed but I decided that I wasn't going to say anything negative about Flyte Tyme, about Prince, Morris, nobody.

That was going to be my first defence – if you can't say anything kind about anybody then don't say anything at all. Everywhere I went – Southside, Northside – everybody seemed to know about this shit and were trying to get me to express how I felt about it.

"Prince done you wrong, man," they'd say.

He did do me wrong, but he didn't know that I still had God on my side. I still understood that God had plans for his children, so I stayed on that path, that lane of having integrity. When you are young black man, most motherfuckers think you don't even know the meaning of the word, let alone possess it.

I had everything intact. The way I was going to fight this situation was not to fight it. I was going to keep pursuing my career. I knew if I said anything it would just belittle me. It would make me sound jealous, that they made it and I didn't.

Some people make it without integrity, and they'll do anything for an opportunity, fuck their friends and family. I am not that kind of guy and won't do those sort of things.

I had confidence in my abilities but it is a hell of pill to swallow when you see your friends on national TV. These were people I had played with six months ago and now they're on the hottest music show around.

Other people have made up their own reasons on why I didn't get the gig with Prince, how I got fired before I got hired. But they don't know the truth. I heard Jimmy Jam get on television once saying I asked Prince to buy me a car, to buy me this and buy me that. I never asked Prince to buy me a goddamned thing 'cos I didn't need Prince to buy me nothing. He didn't need to give me shit. I had money every day, cars, plenty of everything – why did I need him to buy me a motherfucking car?

For me to walk away from Prince must have been a shock for him because, at that time, everything he touched was a success. Everything he asked for he got.

I guess, with me, he thought that I had 100 per cent of nothing. There was him offering me 50 per cent of something and I had the nerve to ask some business questions. The difference between Prince and me was that I don't have the need nor the desire to control people. I just want people to bring their expertise to the party and for everyone to play fair. Prince's way was everyone kiss my ass, everyone suck my dick, you do what the fuck I say, goddamn it, I'm the motherfucker in charge. I don't get on with people like that. I really don't.

I don't regret the whole experience. Even if I had signed with him, I reckon Prince would have let me go after the first album or something because I couldn't let someone I don't respect reign over me. I didn't have respect for Prince. We'd had a bad experience in the past so, from that time, he'd hit my shit list and stayed on it. We were very political in our relationship. When we'd meet each other we'd say "hi" and give each other hugs, the whole nine yards. But inside it was whole different ball game.

I'm thinking, Prince, I got no respect for you because first of all you don't have any respect for the black part of you. You have a white part and a black part, and you only played the black part when it was convenient. You are using all black people for your own ends. You've figured out that you have to manoeuvre yourself in a white world, cater to your white side. I ain't pissed off with that if it brings more to the table, but don't fucking misuse me and don't misuse my people. I am not going along with that.

If me standing up for what I believe in makes me too black for this band or to be in your company, fuck you.

Some people may think it was my use of drugs that Prince didn't like, given that he didn't do drugs, cigarettes, anything like that.

All these great albums, all those great fucking songs, I never recorded any of them sober. Not just some of them, but all of them. I'd never walk in straight and say, "Hi, how are you, let's go to work". There was always at least some marijuana. It was just my lifestyle.

CHAPTER 7
Making it on my own

When the boys in Flyte Tyme walked away, I still felt deep in my heart that success would come. First step was to put a new band together, but this time I wanted to try something different, some rock 'n' roll rather than the R&B and soul that I was used to. As I've said before, the lead singer in a band *is* the band and, just to make sure everyone understood that, this time I called the band Alexander. We'd do covers of songs by the Rolling Stones and Def Leppard and some stuff we wrote ourselves, playing in some clubs I'd not been in before. Looking back, we were a bit ahead of our time – that black rock 'n' roll thing that bands like The BusBoys did later.

It was a great experience. It was fun but it was also an eye opener, as it confirmed that prejudice did exist in the Minneapolis music scene – but it wasn't so much about the colour of your skin but the colour of your dollar. It's about cash. When you're a club owner and you're doing a regular rock 'n' roll club, what are you as a band going to do if you're not playing rock 'n' roll music? How can you get booked at that club? The people who come to that club are rock 'n' roll enthusiasts – they're not R&B enthusiasts.

Unless you can come in and book the club, take the club as a promoter, you ain't going to play. I was one of the few black singers who made it across that divide, one of maybe two to perform in the Twin Cities' white clubs.

Prince and those guys, they were never in the whole music scene in Minneapolis. They never were and they know it. See, white folks would never let us in their scene. They'd let one or two of us in, but do you think they'd let in a whole host of black bands into their white clubs? What are you, crazy? That's like saying you're bringing blacks into the area and they are bringing property values down. It's the same thing with clubs.

I managed to get into that scene when I got a job with The Mystics. I always had the luxury of knowing all these other musicians and other players and people from all walks of life because I played that scene. I think, because this scene didn't admit Prince into it, when he made it he shit right on them. He shit right down their fucking throats. He treated them like shit. He treated all the musicians like shit and he treated the town like shit. Like he was God and you ain't shit. They weren't shit, they weren't on his level but where he had just gone to, some of them had got close. A lot of them had put out albums. I remember this group called DVC: we played with them doing the rock 'n' roll thing. They were a great fucking band and they almost made it. Great groups like Willy and the Bees, the TC Jammers, they could have made it.

I played the real music scene in Minneapolis. I was the black guy in the band who could sing his ass off.

Now I've really got it going off. Everyone's thinking I'm sitting around sad 'cos of the Prince thing, but I ain't sad, I'm getting my thing on.

Rolling Stone asked me to do an interview and like everyone else they wanted to get into the Alexander O'Neal/Prince thing 'cos at this time Prince was in his "no interview" stage.

With that interview I could have taken the opportunity to tell the world what I thought about Prince. *Rolling Stone* was trying to bait me, trying to use me for that purpose. I knew that and I picked up on it quickly. I said, "No dog, if I ain't said anything all this time, what makes you think I am going to give it to you?"

They figured I would be the one to say something really nasty about Prince, but I wouldn't allow it to happen to me. I said it was a good thing for Flyte Tyme, that singers and musicians had two different paths and this was their opportunity and it was right for them to take it.

After the *Rolling Stone* article, now everybody who plays an instrument knows that there was some controversy between Prince and I. They also know that Alexander O'Neal is an entity in the Minneapolis music scene. They all know I've got to be something. What they don't know is the detail about the injustice done to me, but I ain't going to say anything bad about Prince, Terry, Jimmy Jam and the other guys.

The Time was kicking ass and taking names in the world. They were one of the hottest bands ever, ever. They were as hot as firecracker man. They've got Prince backing them, everything going for them. All they've got to do is sit back, keep their mouths shut, kiss Prince's ass and go for the ride. In that order.

After a while, I knew it was time to go back to what I did best, which was R&B. I made the decision that this time around it was to be all about Alexander O'Neal. I'd employ my own musicians. I didn't want to be a member of a band, no more of that shit. There was no sign of a record deal but, at times, I was working for local producers, working in the studio, trying out different things. At one point we put a single out, an uptempo song called "Do You Dare" backed by a ballad called "Playroom", through a Chicago-based label called Erect Records. It did well locally where a lot of people knew me but it never made the national charts.

Two of the regular clubs I played three nights a week were Sylvia on Cedar in Saint Paul and The Chicago Bar in Downtown

Minneapolis. This was when I started getting my style, the ties and the suits, looking sharp. I realized, even at a local level, that you had to have an act, a character that people would want to come and see. I cleaned myself up to look more like a star when I was on the job. We had a lot of fun, they were great times for me, some of my fondest memories.

This period in my life had gone on for about two years and I was on stage in one of the clubs one night not knowing Jimmy Jam and Terry Lewis were in the audience. They were now living in Los Angeles, but they were in town on business and heard I was playing that night. They thought they'd look me up.

I was always spot on with my performances, man. I always gave 150 per cent because I never knew who was in the house. Remember, I always knew I would get a record deal, just never where and when it would come from. I knew if there was such a thing as "I'm going to make it," then it would be me. After Prince and all my friends had got deals, my time would come.

That night I was singing Rick James covers and some great ballads. After the show, Jimmy Jam and Terry came over to talk. After The Time's initial success, life under Prince hadn't turned out quite as they'd expected. Prince, it seemed, didn't allow them to take full credit for all their own work on top of which the band felt they weren't getting their fair share of the money rolling in. Shit, ain't that part of what I had seen coming down the line when Prince had wanted me in the lineup?

Things had come to a head when The Time were due to support Prince at a gig in San Antonio but there was no sign of Jimmy Jam nor Terry. They were stuck by a blizzard back in Atlanta, Georgia, and Prince was forced to play Terry's part on bass – hiding off stage so no one could see him. The mighty Prince was furious and, shortly afterwards, Jimmy Jam and Terry were fired. Monte Moir quit at the same time.

Jimmy Jam and Terry later explained that Prince had told them not to take on any production work for other artists without informing him, but they'd gone ahead and done so anyway. He'd found out they'd just done their first recording with The S.O.S Band with a song called "High Hopes".

Now that The Time was history, Jimmy Jam and Terry were going to go it alone as producers. They said when they got their feet planted firmly in the music industry they were going to come back and get me a deal. And guess what, that's exactly what happened. They became two of the industry's music successful producers and I became a star.

To me, that was a lesson on why to keep your mouth shut. If I'd gone out after the Prince thing, attacking him and Flyte Tyme and just protecting my own ego, saying nasty dirty things about them, do you think they would have helped try and get me a record deal? I don't think so. They never heard Alex say one thing about them, and that's what they remembered. It wasn't easy to keep my mouth shut – that shit isn't easy – but I did.

When they told me they'd try and get me a deal, it was like a light going on. I'd got an iron in the fire. People were helping me. The job now was to keep my shit together, keep singing, keep recording, keep hustling and I'll get there. Most importantly, stay focused, Alex. It's getting close.

I wanted more gigs, more notoriety. I wanted to be recognized as the Number One black R&B artist in Minneapolis and that's what I became. Who's the best singer in town, dog? Well, there's a lot of good ones but there's only one Alexander O'Neal. Everywhere I went in the city to see a show they would invite me up to sing. You don't see that shit anymore. Great singers like Tony Green and his band Westside were great to perform with. Tony could sing a high voice and could sing low. I'd go to his show and he'd come to mine, checking out what new things each of us was doing. It was always fun.

I kept doing my thing, building and building my performances. When the time came I wanted this thing, Alexander O'Neal, to be like a powder keg exploding out of Minneapolis across the whole fucking country. Because that's where things are born, things are born out of nothing. Some of the most significant artists in the world have come to the forefront out of nothing. You wonder, "Where in the hell did they come from?"

At one point I talked to a couple of guys from The Temptations who told me they were looking for a lead singer. I sent them a tape and then called Otis Williams who said he loved my voice but they couldn't hire me because I was too young. The Temptations must have all been in their forties at this point and I was still in my mid-twenties. They'd had another young singer in and it hadn't worked out, so even though I sounded great they didn't want to make the same mistake twice. To be honest, it was probably for the best because there's no way I could have done all that clapping and step-dancing shit.

For a time, not long, I played with a group called Sounds of Blackness who went on to be produced by Jimmy Jam and Terry. The group was led by Gary Hines who became a very good friend of mine. I wasn't with them long because I knew I couldn't do this big gospel thing where I'm just a singer back there in the choir. But what a great experience. Gary taught me a lot about music, about scales, about how to use my voice. I learned a lot from this experience. What a great man to give me some of the best of himself and I do appreciate it so much.

I kept cracking on, just playing doing my things. That era in my life was a wonderful time for me because, for a local guy, I had a nice piece of money in my pocket. I was making nice change every week, which helped with the hustling thing.

My game was this. I'm running a game on a girl and I'm trying to get some Gs, I'm trying to get some dough. I take that money, say I had $1,500, which was a lot of money for a local guy to have, and I'd show it to the girl. I'd say, "I got $1,500 but I need $4,000, so I'm short, can you help me baby?"

I'd get the, "Wow, you're in need, he's in need, he's in need, I got to get this, I got to help him. I got to get this."

So,. "Just do the best you can baby, all right? You're going to help me, do the best you can and if the best you can is two grand that's fine."

"Well honey I couldn't get all of it but I can get you another $1,500."

You know, "Okay that's lovely, baby." That's $1,500 that you're never going to get back.

You can imagine, if a guy has two or three women, and you're running the same game two or three times, then take $1,500 or $1,000 another $1,500, what is that? That's $4,000, isn't it? Plus your $1,500 that you already had, and that's a lot of fucking money for a local guy to be running around with on a Tuesday.

That's how I used to take care of Morris Day. Morris Day and Ollie Wood, and Sue Ann, and all of us. I was the money guy in the crew. See, we had a crew that we used to run together back in those days. They knew I had the money, because I had the game. Because my whole thing was about money, it wasn't about anything else. It wasn't about drugs. I smoked weed, but I didn't do cocaine. It wasn't about no motherfucking drugs – it was about money, money, money.

Then, I used to smoke weed and I liked clothes. Clothes and weed – those were my things. I'm a shoe nut, too, I love shoes. I am definitely a shoe freak. There's a lot of things you can tell by a person's shoes. You can tell who a girl is by her feet. If I look down at a girl's feet, I know what was going on in her head. And, when you're hustling, it's important to know what's going up in a woman's head.

Anyway, I had all the money, because I was the hustler. The other guys, I couldn't understand how they could mess with these girls who are street women and stuff, and not get paid. They just wanted to fuck her because she looked good. I wasn't into just trying to have sex with a good-looking chick. I wanted the chick that I knew that had some clout or could get some money.

If it wasn't that situation, I wasn't going to be fucking around with you. Very seldom would I be messing around to just go and recreationally fuck around. It was a serious business with me, and that's why I would have the money and they didn't. All of my friends, none of them had money, but I did.

Still, I got to the point where I stopped using those kinds of games. Eventually, I just started telling the motherfuckers straight off the bat, "This is where I'm coming from, and this is what it is. If you ain't about this shit here, if you ain't about what I'm about, then let's just not do this. If you ain't up to this, then this is a waste of your time. If I'm hustling my ass off in every way to make my life, to get to where I need to get to, then I'm not going to accept any less from you. If you're going to be with me, and be hanging with me, then this is what it is. And, if this scares you, then go away."

CHAPTER 8
Prime time

I'm at home one morning, blasting my music, smoking my weed, when Terry Lewis calls me on the phone. First thing he said was, "Go turn that music down, nigger." First I got put off when he said that, like who was this motherfucker to call my house and tell me to turn my damn music down? Still, I did as he asked. Despite the Prince shit, Terry was still my friend, and I have got a lot of respect for him.

He said, "Look here man, we've got a deal for you." Right then and there I knew it was on.

I never would have got that phone call if I had bad-mouthed the guys from Flyte Tyme or Prince. I had counted on my integrity, hard work and perseverance to all come together to launch me to a national level at some point.

I had never known who the deal was going to come from. Jimmy Jam and Terry had been to places I hadn't. They'd been in offices dealing with executive motherfuckers in Los Angeles. At this stage, I hadn't been there. I hadn't never dealt with motherfuckers like that, big players, heavy hitters.

It was my great fortune that Terry and Jimmy Jam had ended up working with Tabu Records, which was owned by the great Clarence Avant. Clarence was already a legend in the industry having managed the likes of Bill Withers, Sarah Vaughan and Jimmy Smith.

Clarence had set up Tabu Records and signed to the label people like the S.O.S. Band and Cherrelle. Jimmy and Terry had been hired to produce the S.O.S. Band's fourth album and it was while recording this that they'd been struck by the blizzard that grounded their flight, missing the performance with The Time for which Prince had fired them. Fate.

Turns out Jimmy and Terry had been working with a singer, I think called Jeffrey Robinson, but for some reason he didn't work out. Now they were looking for someone to take his place, subject to final approval by Clarence. Now all the pieces finally slotted into place. They could have given the deal to anyone they wanted but I got the call and Terry invited me out to their studio in Bloomington, Minnesoat, about 10 miles south of Minneapolis.

I was coming into a part of the record industry that was huge and going places. I was impressed with Clarence. It was my time around a black man that had that type of clout in him, that type of prestige within not only the industry but in so many things like fundraisers. Also, the things he did for his friends, people like Quincy Jones and the Motown CEO Jheryl Busby, who were his best friends.

These are the kind of people that I was now associating with. These names are so big, these people so big and here is this little boy from Mississippi.

When I first met Quincy Jones, I was honoured to be in his presence and honoured to meet him. But, in all honesty, I was finding my way around the industry and I always kept my eyes open. I always kind of thought that they'd better look out for me. That's what I felt like. It felt like, "Alex, you know what? You're a bad motherfucker man, you're a bad dude." It wasn't because I was believing my own hype or anything like that – it was because I had a clear vision. God had placed a clear vision in my mind of how I'd got to go where I got to. How I got the deal. Out of all those singers in Minneapolis, out of all those musicians, a lot of them singers and shit wouldn't give me the time of the day.

What they didn't realize is that I paid my dues in the Twin Cities in the local music scene just as much as any musician or any singer. I paid my dues, hardcore. While we was out hustling on the street and doing all this stuff, getting our hustle on and shit, I still was going to work three nights a week.

The difference between me and the guys I hustled with was that I had vision in me. I wanted something and they didn't. If they had a dream, an idea, then they were not doing anything about it. They were content getting older, still hustling girls but the girls are getting younger. That shit's old, it's got a shelf life. These guys, they let the game catch them up. I used the game to get to the next level. That's all I did once I figured out that I could do this, that I could really do music.

I'd learn over time that shit happens so fast in the music industry you've got to take it while it's happening. Everybody is going to get fucked eventually, you've just got to find out how much fucking you can take. You're definitely going to get screwed at some point.

Tabu Records offered me $10,000 front money but I recorded the whole of that first album, *Alexander O'Neal*, before I got one quarter. But I never did it for the damn front money. If it had been $50,000 or $100,000 – which, of course, I'd never seen at that time in my life – it would still have been about getting the deal, getting out there. I had a perception of how I thought it would be because of the way that they lived from their stint at being out there at that level. But I had the beauty and luxury of not having to deal with bands and stuff 'cos I had a solo deal. I'm the man and the commodity. That's a beautiful thing.

All of the guys in The Time ended up being involved in the Alexander O'Neal project. They were producers, my band, my family. They worked me to death and I worked myself to death and I loved it.

I'd ended up with the band that Prince had put together, but with no Prince. It's all in my name. Is that nice or is that nice? Jimmy Jam and Terry, Monte Moir and Jellybean Johnson – all these guys were writing Alexander O'Neal's songs. Wow, what a turnaround.

All these guys that had all that notoriety, the whole country going The Time crazy, they turn into record producers now and they're helping me. Everything The Time, Jimmy Jam and Terry Lewis touches turns to gold. Everything. In the industry in my era, you had to have the total package. You had to be good looking, be sellable, a commodity. I think I had it all, talent, looks, articulate. I was ready for that deal. I was primed and ready.

I think Terry and Jimmy had other motivations for getting me that deal. I suspect it was because Prince had slapped them in the face and they'd slapped him back by getting me the deal and helping to make me a star.

From what I understand they weren't making no money out there on the road as The Time. The change they were getting was a drop in the bucket compared to what Prince was putting in his pocket. He wrote all their first album, they didn't write shit, so they weren't going to get shit. All the songwriting royalties went to Prince.

But what they did get was a foundation for their career, more than they would have got sitting on their ass at home saying, "No, we're not going to take this deal with Prince 'cos it will hurt someone's feelings." Mine, specifically, because I was being left behind. For them, it was the right thing to do. You can't turn opportunity down when it knocks on your door – that could be your only shot. That's why I always kept my eyes open for my chance. I never knew where it was going to come from, but I knew it was going to happen.

Musically I had really enjoyed the time that I'd been on my own as it was a period for me in my life where it just pushed me to another level. Seeing them, The Time, with all their success, it just made me "up my game" in the Minneapolis and Saint Paul area. I started setting certain protocols for myself in order to be in the right place, the right frame of mind.

I would look at people who had success in the music industry and I started conducting myself like them. I'd be working as hard as I could and devoting myself to the music as much as was possible. With the bands I was playing with, I also hoped that success would come for them as well. I wanted to take some of them with me but, as it turned out, that didn't happen. These were guys like John Rivers and Ben Locket, my drummer and my keyboard player. John and I wrote my first record together, "Playroom" / "Do You Dare". After I got the deal, I was excited so I was talking to them about it and telling them to stick with me, but I think that, for some reason, they were intimidated.

Sometimes your friends wish you well and hope for your success, but in fact they were pretty shocked that I'd actually gone and done it. It's like they felt like I had walked away from them but they had actually walked away from me. I didn't know how to take that because I was like, "I want to take you all with me. You're my band. You're going to be the band director. You're going to do this thing." But I don't know if they really believed. I don't think I even saw them again because I got word that they were spreading some not so not-so-kind rumours about me, telling my personal business, telling stuff that shouldn't have been told.

I'll never forget that I went over to play my new album to a good friend of mine, a drummer from Minneapolis named Bobby Vandell. I love Bobby Vandell. He is a good friend, but I don't think he could handle the fact that I had a deal. He was getting ready for a gig and he was too damn busy putting his drums and stuff together to listen to my album. He couldn't handle it. I had a lot of that shit going on around me.

A lot of times people hate to see you change. They didn't want to see me change. They didn't want that to happen, perceiving how they thought my whole life had changed tremendously.

When my shot came from Jimmy Jam and Terry, I didn't go with "Let me see the contract, let's negotiate this." We did it ass backwards because of our friendship, because of the trust. I didn't have the knowledge to get myself a fancy California lawyer who'd been in the music industry to go through the deal and stuff. I had this guy from Minneapolis representing me but neither he nor I had the knowledge we needed, so we made a lot of concessions. I had to decide myself that this is the deal: whether it's good, bad or indifferent it's going down. Most importantly, once again, I decided to trust in God that this is my time. And guess what? It obviously was. God had his hand all over this.

When we finished the album, simply titled *Alexander O'Neal*, and presented it to Clarence, his reaction was, "Where's this guy been all my life? This guy's phenomenal. This guy's great." I will never forget that.

When the album was released, we had a smash on our hands. One of the tracks, "Innocent", went to No. 11 on the Billboard R&B chart right off the bat. Shit, I had a national hit record off my first album.

The reason I think we got a big hit was because "Innocent" sounded so similar to the first record released by The Time, "Get It Up". Shit, they could have been first cousins, cut out of the same thing. Other great songs on the album included "If You Were Here Tonight", "A Broken Heart Can Mend" and "What's Missing". The album went gold and "Innocent" on its own sold more than half a million copies. In the UK alone, where I was to win a lasting audience, we sold more than 100,000 copies.

As it turned out, I'd had the No. 1 producers in the country working with me. Just over a year later, Jimmy Jam and Terry ended up winning a Grammy as Producers of the Year. My album was important in earning them the award but I wasn't the only artist they'd worked with that year: they'd also produced huge hits for the likes of Janet Jackson, Patti Austin, The S.O.S Band and the Human League. Their triumph, though, was immense considering that they were up against the likes of Prince and Michael Jackson. Not bad for two black boys from Minneapolis.

I was the first name they called when they gave their thanks after picking up the award. They said they wanted to thank Alexander O'Neal, and they gave me the love. This was on national TV and I'm sitting at home thinking, yeah, we got your asses, we got your asses now. It was like I'd won a Grammy myself.

Some time later, I saw Prince for the first time since getting the deal. We were both in this club, Carlos And Charlie's on Sunset Boulevard in Los Angeles. Every Monday night anybody who was anybody would come there. Prince was there with Big Chick, his blonde bodyguard, and I walked over. Chick got up in my face but Prince said no, it's cool. He invited me to sit down and congratulated me on the album. We talked for a few minutes and it was okay. I got up and went back to my party.

I was with people from Sony Records and CBS, powerful boys. Shit, this was so different to the first time I'd come to LA and no one would give me the time of day.

The only downside of the success of the first album was that I didn't get a goddamn thing out of it. Everyone else got all the money, I got the career. But that's what the singer gets – you've just come into the game and don't know the rules. I was fortunate that my first album was followed by a second success, then a third. Most guys don't even get a successful first album. It's very difficult to have just one hit in your whole career. We were fortunate. We were on a roll.

We set a whole new tone in the music industry as well 'cos this was the start of the video era. There was also Black Entertainment Television (BET): if you got on rotation on that, then the whole country would know who the fuck you are 'cos it's the only damn black station we've got. MTV was there but it was still mostly just rock.

After the first album was released, we went on tour. I'd get paid $30,000 here or $50,000 there and, by the end of the year, I had probably made about half a million dollars. Shit, I worked my ass off for 16 months promoting that album with our distributors, CBS. It takes a lot of work to have a hit record. You've got to be willing to roll up your damn sleeves and work, work, work. We had to get on planes, be there. I remember we went to Washington DC, the first city on the tour, and they spoiled me rotten. Shit, the guy from CBS was buying me cocaine with his company credit card. We were in the CBS machine. When I see people today like Chris Brown getting themselves in trouble, I know that feeling. I've been there.

The highlight at that point in time for me was winning Chicago. I don't have the same passion for New York as I do for the Windy City, maybe it's because I lived there. I think though it's because Chicago is one of the most hospitable cities that I have been in my life. Certainly, in the United States, it is the most hospitable to me. Its people are so humble and accommodating.

At times I'd fly up there at the weekend from Minneapolis and hang out with Michael Jordan and all those guys, we were all friends. Michael, he used to come to my gigs and I did his birthday party. We started kicking it. If you're a black man in Chicago and you're at that level, you've got it going on. I just had the best of Chicago – and, believe me, the best of Chicago is good.

By the time of the second album, *Hearsay*, the deal changes. I'm getting around $100,000 front money but now the extra payments for concerts and stuff are in six figures. I'm getting paid, but I'm also playing hard. When we did the first record, I had been smoking weed forever and snorting coke occasionally. There'd be days and days when I'm taking care of business and I haven't thought about coke. I hadn't reached that point where I *had* to have it. But, by the time of the second album in 1987, coke is not occasional. It's happening big time. To me, snorting coke is recreational. It's child's play compared with smoking it or shooting it. When you smoke cocaine, the whole thing is a different game.

For me, these were the start of the good times but not everyone was celebrating my success, especially some of people that I'd been hanging out with back in Minneapolis. They couldn't stand seeing my success because, to them, I was just a hustler – just like them – and now here I was, hitting the big time. They'd forgotten I'd told them, "The difference between you and me is that I have a goal in life. I'm hustling for something, whereas you're just hustling for the game. I'm hustling because I want to be a recording artist, a singer, a star. I got to hustle to pay for studio time. I got to hustle to make something happen. You guys are hustling just to put it in your pocket, to go shopping, pose up and go on to the next hustle. This singing thing I'm doing three nights a week in these clubs is really going to lead up to something. You don't see it but I do. You would never know what to do with it because it isn't your destiny. I am going to go to a level that Minneapolis had never seen in a black man like me."

Around some of these people who purported to be my friends, I had to be careful. I remember one time having a load of money at the house, maybe 300 or 400 thousand dollars. I told Janet, my girlfriend and road manager, to stash it at her place. In the city I didn't want that kind of money in the house 'cos I got people staying round who would try and steal everything they could because they thought I was finished with them. They'd take $5,000 and run off, say, to Philadelphia. I could have had a lot of these motherfuckers killed, but I didn't want to carry that burden. I don't want to answer to God for that. I don't want to have to deal with that in the afterlife. You are going to meet Him. You bet your ass you're going to meet Him.

Terry and Jimmy, I think, also had some unfinished business with Minneapolis – particularly how the city had treated its black musicians, keeping all but one or two of us out of their white clubs. Even though I'd had access to those clubs, because my white friends and peers all knew how talented I was and everything else, they were always making more money than I was.

Did I now want to make their asses pay, too? Sure I did. Now I've got a national deal, what are you going to say, bitch? Now what you going to do 'cos y'all motherfuckers are going to get it California-style, New York City-style, baby. I'm going to roll on all of you so hard that y'all ain't going to know what hit you.

I got the money, the cars, the girls. That's my attitude.

Guess what, you know why I'm going to hit y'all hard? Because you cocksuckers are a bunch of player-hating non-believers. I told y'all through my behaviour that this was jumping off, I told y'all that I was that guy, not just some scum out here on the street. I told you that.

So, when I got my deal, it kind of broke Minneapolis. It broke their face, cracked their face wide open. I'm like, now who's running this shit, who's the boss, who's the man now? I acted just like that. I bought two fucking big-ass Mercedes at the same time, along with a Corvette and a truck.

People on a local level talk like they know you, but just because you say "hi" and "bye" to somebody doesn't mean you know them or they know you. They didn't give a shit before, now I'm at a level where I don't give two fucks about what you think or say about me but I'm still going to be kind to your ass. I'm going to be cool.

I ain't going to be like Prince. I ain't going to walk into a place surrounded by bodyguards. I ain't going to be standoffish, looking around a place like you're scared to death of everybody. What the fuck are you scared of? The day I start being afraid of my own people – the day I stop being a black man – I'll let you know.

It's like people whispering, "When you reach a certain level there's places you shouldn't go, certain people you shouldn't be with. You shouldn't be with poor people, in the black community because you're above that."

But I'm a black man, who came up with that shit?

"Well, ain't that the way Prince acts? Ain't that the way Michael acts? Ain't that where Lionel's at?"

They're saying that, if you want to have a possibility of going to the next level you definitely don't want to be a black, black man. You have to be a white, black man.

That was the time when I maintained myself as a black man and I was proud of myself. I lived in an area of the country that got me prepared for the white man's world. There are a lot of cities in the United States where you don't interact with white people, which means the only thing you know is a stereotype. All you know is what someone tells you. If you're in West Chicago or Harlem, all your reactions will be with black people or people of colour. The only whites you see are sitting behind the wheel of a police car.

In Minneapolis and Saint Paul you will soon learn shit about other races that you didn't know, and you will welcome it. The Twin Cities taught me how to deal with people. You can't go around hating people just 'cos of the colour of their skin. Even though I came out of that red, black and green type of Black Consciousness thing, Minneapolis helped me to change my views.

You don't know what white families do, you have never slept in a house with a white family, never shared a meal with a white family, you don't know that they ain't no different than you. If you live in somewhere like Minneapolis, Denver or, say, Seattle, it opens your eyes. Not everywhere, though. In my experience, folks on the West Coast are big-time racist bastards. They're so full of shit out in California. It's the most racist state in the goddamn Union. They hide behind some shit but there are some nigger-hating motherfuckers out there. They got all kinds of hate groups out there.

Through all the hustling and everything else, I am still a good man. That's what a lot of people didn't understand – they thought that I'm this motherfucker hustling kind of fella and that I must be a bad person. No, I've got a good heart. I'm still giving. I still care about my mother and family. I care about people.

Getting the deal didn't change that.

CHAPTER 9

Wedding rings and white powder

So life is good. I've finally got the record deal I'd been chasing for years, the money is starting to pour in and there's more girls on the scene than I can cope with. What do you do next? You get married of course.

I'd met this beautiful Swedish-American girl called Debbie Weston. Straight off she was my kind of woman and I instantly had a lot of love for her. After we'd spent our first night together, I think we both knew that this was not just a one-night stand or that kind of thing. I could tell that she was special to me. She had her own baggage – she was coming off a divorce at the time we met. She'd been married to a doctor or something like that. I guess it was time for her to move on.

Just because I did my own thing and behaved the way I did, the hustling, I did know how to behave if I wanted a relationship. I knew how to be special, to be very special.

She didn't know nothing about me – she just knew what I showed her.

Before the year was out, we flew to Las Vegas and got married, which was very, very heart-wrenching for all these women in Minneapolis who were in my scene. That was a hell of a pill for them to swallow – I hadn't chosen any of them, I'd chosen Debbie, someone they didn't know anything about. I think that was one of the things that attracted me to Debbie – that she wasn't in the Minneapolis scene.

She was new. She was a suburbanite. It was something new, a challenge.

I used to pride myself on taking girls that would never do this or that and I would "turn them out", but for Debbie that wasn't going to be the case because she was my wife.

Unfortunately, from the start, I wasn't a good husband. She never had me to herself, ever. I was always, for a long time, playing the field. I had children during the marriage with other women. Debbie knew when we got married that I'd had a son, Carlton, with my Tasha. Carlton was four years old at the time, and he was everything to me. To me he came before any woman, anybody, anywhere. He lived with Tasha but, in reality, he spent most of his time with me and Debbie.

I tried to keep the two sides of my life separate but all the girls I would see knew I was married. For them that was no big deal. I had my priorities all screwed up. I equated being a good man, a good husband and a good father to simply being a good provider. I have learned since then it takes a lot, lot more.

I was also still abusive, very abusive physically. I was still carrying that baggage and hadn't yet learned that abuse had no place in a marriage. I think Debbie was afraid of me after she found out how violent I could be.

We were living in Apple Valley, Dakota County, about 20 miles south of Minneapolis, in a lovely two-bedroom apartment off a golf course. I really loved that place because, when I was home, I worked out a lot. It was great for me to go for walks and runs, a place where I could think and do all kinds of stuff.

The marriage was good for quite some time and I was so happy when, about a year after we got married, she told me she was pregnant. My daughter Harmony was soon born and two years later along came her sister, Alexandra.

I loved Debbie to bits, I really did. I think for some time, quite a while, she loved me. She expressed to me that she thought this was the one, that we'd be together forever and I thought that, too. I had a lovely life at home and I think she adored me at that time.

Plus we had a lot of money. Money kept rolling in, lots of it. The more money, the more drugs. More money, more isolation to do the drugs. With more money I'm really not going to stop what I'm doing now, it's on, it's happening. This is money I am earning. These were big days but the really big days were yet to come.

I kept running around, that was my M.O. The black girls in Minneapolis would say "don't mess with him, girl, because he don't mess with nothing but white girls". Black girls, they don't like that. They see that, the first time you get some success, the first thing you do is go get a white girl. They hate it.

I'd be out doing my thing and I'd come home after being up for five days straight. As far as I was concerned, nobody better say anything to me about where I'd been and what I'd been doing – that's way out of your jurisdiction. Shows you how warped my thinking was. This was my wife.

I'd come home after doing drugs, cocaine, there were no questions to me, it was all sweetness and kindness. I'd have breakfast, go to bed and when I wake up, it was on again. I am getting dressed, getting cleaned up and it's, "I'll see you when I see you". Once again, what I do out there at night ain't got nothing to do with you. Ain't no one I'm running with going to bring it to Debbie, tell her what I'm doing, 'cos she's living way out in the suburbs. You might think there's something going on but you don't see it, you don't hear about it.

Eventually, though Debbie did hear something about what I

had been up to. Somehow she found out I'd flown an old girlfriend, Avery, from Los Angeles to Minneapolis to spend a few days with me. Debbie did the one thing she said she'd never do and walked out with the kids.

I don't blame her or not blame her. I am not trying to glorify anything that passed over. I guess she was getting a sense then that I like the ladies and, the more stardom I got, the prettier the girls became.

To me at the time Debbie walking out confirmed what I felt then, that no woman could be trusted. I don't believe a damn thing when women tell me what they won't do because that is the biggest crock of bullshit I have ever heard. I have experienced this several times in different relationships.

After a while, I persuaded Debbie to come home and everything is fine for a while as I made things right. But again my attitude was still that this was my business, it hasn't got a damn shit to do with you, you are taken care of. It seems crazy now but, even though Debbie was home, I never stopped seeing Avery. She was stunning.

It wasn't until later that I found out how Debbie felt. She felt that she'd never had me to herself, ever. How true was that? She had everything but me. Now, man, that is a hell of a lot of abuse for anyone to take. Given how things were I suppose it was no surprise that Debbie gravitated to Harmony who became her best friend. Everything became about the two of them.

I never told Debbie I was never going to do that again or anything like that. I never had that kind of conversation. I could have been the kind of star, the kind of man to say, "You know what, I want a divorce. I don't want to be with you anymore." But I never ever felt that way about Debbie. I was one of those men who had his cake and ate it too. I ate too much cake.

I kept doing my thing but as I kept doing so it was apparent that after a while she was sliding her own way around. I don't know if she reacted to anything I was doing in reference to having an affair or anything like that. That didn't even cross my mind 'cos I figured I had her on lockdown. She had my baby. I am Alexander O'Neal, the star, where is she going? She ain't going nowhere. Well, when things got bad, I think people around probably convinced her my career was over, that I was getting really reckless.

My use of cocaine at this time, with the money pouring in as my career started to take off, had reached the point where I was spending up to $1,000 a day buying gear. I'd have three or four different dealers coming to the house every day. By this time we'd moved out of the suburbs and back into the city, a lovely three-storey place where I had the attic area to myself where I could do my stuff.

It was all these dealers coming to the place that got me in shit with the FBI. I'd be lying in bed at night and I'd be woken up by the sound of the trash cans being turned over. At the time I thought it was raccoons or something. In fact, it was the FBI searching through my trash in search of paraphernalia, all kind of drugs shit. They'd thought I was the dealer, not the buyer.

Sure enough, the day came when the FBI came into the house, looking for me but there was only Debbie at home. After they'd done a search of the place and found 300 tablets of Valium in the master bedroom, they dragged her off to jail. While all this was going on, I'd been with another woman but eventually I got a call from my attorney who told me what the situation was. I jumped in my Corvette and shot home real quick. I wasn't afraid of no damn FBI but they had left by the time I got there.

The FBI were on a mission. They seized my bank accounts and tried to accuse me of being a drug dealer, that was their whole thing. But it was just bullshit. They knew damn well I just had so much money and they couldn't stand it. Here I am rolling through Minneapolis like I'm untouchable. I am being real crazy rolling around in a beige 650 Mercedes-Benz. I am hot and I am legal and it is driving them crazy. I am not like the other stars coming out of Minneapolis. I am your worst nightmare and your worst daymare, too. I don't like the police, and I don't like what you all stand for. And, guess what? All of you can kiss my ass. That was my attitude.

Y'all aren't going to get me 'cos I'm motherfucking too fast for y'all.

Of course, the FBI had no case against me. Sure I was using cocaine but I was never a dealer. They had to release my bank accounts but, when they did so, of the $79,000 I had in there I only got $33,000 back. I could have taken them to court to get the rest back, to make a stink. But here's the thing you might want to think about if you want to take the police to court. Okay, they'll think, take us to court, but the next time we come in your house, we might plant a kilo of cocaine somewhere. I know how police are, especially in America. If they want you bad enough, they will get your ass. That was my thing, I know how they think. If I was going to show them up, then they were going to show me, and I didn't want that. I am still doing my drugs, still doing my thing, still making a shitload of money.

In two days after the FBI backed off I had managed to get $40,000 from different friends who advanced me money. It was my way of showing the FBI and the cops couldn't stop me.

Not long after this, Debbie left me a second time. She took my girls and went down to Florida and the bitch took $100,000 with her. I went crazy trying to find her.

Eventually, many years later, I found a way to get through to her and that was with my album, *All True Man*. The songs on the album were powerful, with stuff like, "Baby, let's hang on, hang on". It had all types of appeal if you were having problems like ours in a relationship. I didn't know where Debbie was but I knew somehow she'd hear the songs and get the message. Sure enough she surfaced and I said, "Baby, come home, just bring the girls and come home." And they did.

Whether in a good marriage or bad, this shit happens.

She had this attorney I ended up dealing with and he didn't like me. He couldn't stand me. He wanted to get me, hurt me because I wouldn't let him finish negotiating for a series of concerts I was to do at London's Wembley Arena. I'd realized he didn't know what the fuck he was doing. He was a corporate lawyer from Minneapolis, dealt with a lot of shit but, just because you're smart, that doesn't mean you know the showbusiness game. He did not know the fucking game. I brought in two cats I knew in Chicago instead and they brought a lot of shit to the table. The bad thing about it is I got fucked by the guys I'd brought in and Debbie was to do something for which I have never been able to forgive her. I gave these guys $50,000 and, on top of that, they got $35,000 for a video shoot I did and which I didn't know they had been paid. What drove me mad though was that somehow they persuaded Debbie to give them another $50,000.

Look at how much these guys got. I wasn't going to give them anything more than $50,000 in total, tell them "Fuck you, that's it. You motherfuckers come out of Chicago and you ain't got a pot to piss in or a window to throw it out of before I brought you in."

From that point on that's when the monster came out. I loved Debbie but I hated her. I didn't want to kill her but I wanted to make her as miserable as I fucking possibly could, every second. Every time I looked at her I was disgusted.

I don't know what those guys said to make her give them that money but my guess is these motherfuckers told her I was going to leave her for Janet Thompson, who was my kind of road manager/ valet/all kinds of shit and also my girl. I had brought Janet from Toronto. I'd been there to play a gig and afterwards the promoters took me to a club. I saw this big sexy blonde, and I love voluptuous women like this. Janet was big and sexy and blonde and I like that. We started talking and straight off I said, "Go pack your bags, you're going to be my tour manager." We spent the night just talking, no sex. That came months down the line. Eventually we had a child together, a daughter Fate.

What Debbie had done in London had fucked her up and fucked me up, too. When we got back to the States every time I looked at her, I wanted to punch her out and, sometimes I did. I just despised her.

When she did eventually leave me for good she actually did me a favour 'cos she could have killed me. As abusive as I was, she could have killed me. If you beat a dog so long, how do you think that dog is ever going to trust you? After all the beatings, the violence, there was no shit that she did that caused all that, that was just my response.

I do regret doing that. I regret it dearly. And, to her and to the whole world, I do apologize and I hope to make amends about that whole experience. It was really horrible and it hurts me today to think that, as good a man as I am, that I could actually possess that type of behaviour.

We were married for years after Wembley. We moved to Vegas after the FBI broke into the house 'cos I didn't want to stay in Minneapolis no more. It continued on, the drugs, the beatings.

It would be another nine years before she decided that she'd had enough.

CHAPTER 10
Boston

I'd arrived. Hit record, money rolling in, everything laid out on a plate. When you get in a position like this, you think it will last forever, and that nothing could spoil the dream you're living. Well, my own recklessness and a massive amount of cocaine nearly ruined everything.

I'd flown to Boston, Massachusetts with Debbie and the girls to do some promotional work for the first album. I'd settled them into our suite at the hotel and then headed out with the local promoters and record company officials.

Debbie would never question what I was doing and where I went, that was none of her business. I didn't know how to be a husband at that time. I was just getting this thing jump-started and was going to do whatever I wanted, like always.

That night I'd done a show somewhere in town, and afterwards one of the guys working with the promoters took me and some others back to his loft apartment. We're chilling out, snorting some coke. Later, as we're getting ready to leave and wind down, I went back to the hotel and one of the guys decided to send me a little present, which was a girl. He asked if I liked her and I said sure, she's okay, and he gave her to me as a "Welcome to Boston" fucking present.

Now I've got Debbie and the girls upstairs, but that doesn't mean shit to me at that time. I'd always book another room in a hotel for just such an occasion as was happening now.

We went back to the hotel, and up to the room I'd booked but it all went bad, and the next morning the girl was crying rape.

Something happened in that room that I'm not proud of, but it wasn't rape. That's why I'm sitting here today and I never got charged with anything like that. If they did any kind of vaginal testing, anything like that, they weren't going to find anything because there wasn't a rape.

That didn't happen, I never penetrated her. What I did was get so fucking pissed off that the bitch had been there all night doing my drugs, doing the shit, we all whacked the fuck out and it's about 7 or 8 o'clock in the morning and she decided she's getting ready to go. What? Bitch crazy. You must be out of your fucking mind. Then I smacked her around a little bit. I was trying to do some sex things with her but it wasn't happening, so I just got frustrated and said, "Fuck this".

I smacked her around a little bit and then, I think, there was the humiliation of the attempt of trying to do some sex things. She did some things but she didn't do it the way I liked it done. I'm from Minneapolis, goddamn it, the way we roll, she didn't do it the way I wanted it done. We never got to having sex. Oral sex, yes, but that wasn't forced. I said something happened, but it wasn't damn rape. After a little bit of oral sex, I'm like, "Dog, you don't want to have sex with somebody that doesn't want to have sex with you, okay."

That's number one. I'm not used to that but, being coked out of my motherfucking head and her being coked out of her head, I got mad. When I got mad, then I got out of control. That's when I slapped her up twice, or something, and I wouldn't let her leave. She couldn't talk me into letting her go, I had to decide to let her go. When I did decide to let her go, she went straight to the police. I guess she was getting me for slapping her up and she called it rape.

The next thing I know I've got two detectives looking for me at the hotel. But they were very kind, man, they were kind and they took care of me, these two white detectives. They said, "We don't want to make a scene." And this, that, and the other. And they were cool, the way they handled this shit.

They took me down to the station and Debbie came with me. What the fuck could she say? Nothing. She was hurt and it was embarrassing. It was a very difficult time for both of us.

After the police station there was arraignment hearing set. Luckily for me, I got hold of this great lawyer, William O'Hara, one of those attorneys who hang out at the Court House and give out their cards. It was great having an Irish attorney in an Irish city. It was like God had sent William to me, I needed that. I went to an arraignment just to see if they carried the case any further but they made no decision at that time so I went back home. I'm embarrassed, I'm hurting, any man telling you he wouldn't be embarrassed by an allegation like that is a damn liar.

As you'd expect, this shit was all over the news. All of a sudden the dream had turned into a nightmare. My heart was broken.

I will always be grateful to the people who stood by me at that time, chief among them being Clarence Avant.

Clarence, such a powerful man, just said to me, "Look, I don't want you sitting up worrying yourself to death, going crazy about this allegation. We're going to make sure everything is fine. We are going to fix this. Whatever it takes, I don't give a damn if it takes $100,000 or $200,000 or $300,000, or whatever, this is going to get dealt with, okay?"

Another friend at that time who really stood by me was Randall Sanders, but we haven't seen each other since then. I love him to death and he's my dear friend, he's a very godly man and he helped me to walk through that situation when I was at my weakest point.

So, I had the support of Clarence and Randall. I didn't need the support of anybody else. I had his promise here and his thing, but a lot of the country didn't get it and seemed to want me to be guilty.

Being accused of rape, that shit gets up in your head, man. You can't eat, you can't sleep, you can't do a goddamn thing because everybody, all the people in your world knew that this is going down.

The reaction from a lot of people in Minneapolis was very difficult to take.

Minneapolis really loved this one – they'd eat it up. The Twin Cities turned their back on me and shit all over me. Them motherfuckers, the black radio station was saying, "Yes, nigger got your bitch ass now, motherfucker." Boy, they just ran it and, boy, they smeared me and made sure that everybody knew that I got accused of rape in Boston.

You got all these people and they all believe you did it. I went to a club, an interracial club, and a white girl said, "Hey, you raped any white girls lately?" Man, I'm like, "See, a bitch like you, you don't even know, you don't have a clue but all you need is an ass whooping. You need a motherfucker to take you and show you how much power you really got, bitch, okay? First of all, you got your information wrong. You didn't care if she was white, black, blue or green. It wasn't no white girl, it was a black girl. Okay? It wasn't no white girl."

That's the kind of humiliation I went through. Talking to one of my friends, he said, "See, most people, they think you're guilty, man, they think you did that." Why the fuck do I have to rape a bitch? That's not my M.O, anyone who knows me will confirm that.

But, until the court came to a decision, I couldn't exonerate

Left and above:
Alex, aged around nine,
during his childhood
days in Natchez,
Mississippi

Right: Alex's father,
also called Alexander
O'Neal, who died
just a few months
before Alex was born

Left: Graduation day from high school in Natchez. It was Alex's football skills rather than academic success that won him a place at college

Above: Alex's sister, Dot

Right: Flyte Tyme days with Alex up front and Terry Lewis on guitar

Above: Alex performing in Stockport in 2016

Above: Alex at Lake Calhoun in Minneapolis. A chance meeting in one of the city's parks ignited his whole career

Above, left: Alex (left) with his mother Dora (front row, centre) and sister Faye (front row, right). Back row from left: brother Larrie, Faye's then husband Robert and Alex's cousin Cornell Washington. **Above, right, top:** Alex barbecuing. **Above, right, below:** Alex with his great friend Mike Mackell with whom he created The Soul Morticians

Above: What the 1980s was all about – style

Above: Alex, seated, backstage with the legendary Jimmy Jam (left)

Above: Alex, centre, with his cousin Clarence Bear Anderson, left, and drummer Rodney Jenkins

Above: Promoting another album. The work never stopped

Above: Photo shoot for his own band, Alexander

Left: Alex, backstage

Below: By the mid-'80s the money is just pouring in for Alex...

Left: Okay, not all of Alex's fashion statements hit the right mark

Below: Alex promoting the *Hearsay* album

Above: Alex with friends, celebrating the success of his 1985 debut album

Left: Photo shoot
for the *All True Man*
album, 1991

Above: With Alexander, the band Alex created and named after himself

Above: Alex with Cherrelle, a great singer and his great friend

Above: Alex's daughter Faith Thompson, pictured aged three at a friend's wedding

Left: Alex, on top of the world, in 1987

Above: The hits keep coming – Alex relaxing in the offices at Tabu Records

Above: In the studio with Steve Hodges, left, and Terry Lewis, complete with hat

Above: On stage Alex always gives it his all – every night is a new challenge

Left: With Cynthia in London for the Wembley Arena gigs in December 1989. At the time she was just his dancer but he already knew that she was something special

Above: Alex with his daughter, Alexandra

Above: Alex with Cynthia, downtime during a rehearsal

Clockwise, from above left: Alex's son Carlton; sister Patricia; daughter Harmony

Above: Alex's little princesses, Louisa, left, and Siana

Left: Alex with Cynthia, 2016

Below: Entering the *Celebrity Big Brother* house, January 2015

Above: Alex's daughter Cassandra TeLea, who has also inherited his incredible voice

Right: Alex talking to Emma Willis before his *Celebrity Big Brother* stint in 2015

myself. In a situation like that, the best thing to do is keep your mouth shut, be quiet. I knew the truth of what had happened. I had hit the girl, which was wrong, but there was no rape and I had to pray the court would see the truth.

My friend Donald Ray called me about 7am on a Friday. He woke me up out of a dead sleep and he said, "Get on the phone, man, have you read the papers? They threw that shit out in Boston, man, they threw that shit." I jumped about dancing and shouting, "Yes, you motherfuckers, now."

Let me make this perfectly clear – had I had done what that girl accused me of, I would have deserved every punishment that sort of crime merits. But it didn't happen, and she knows it didn't happen.

You know when people are telling the truth and when they are lying. Like when Mike Tyson got up in that black church in Atlanta and said, "I'm innocent, I did not rape that girl, I'm innocent, that's it." Right then and there I said, "You see Mike? That motherfucker is going to the penitentiary." I'm sitting there watching and I'm saying, "Your black ass is going to the penitentiary." Guess where he went? To a penitentiary, because he was guilty and you knew it the second he opened his mouth.

With my innocence established there were all those people in Minneapolis to deal with who had tried to do me down, who'd hoped to see me destroyed. Now, they got to pay. They got to pay for me seeing the hatred in their eyes. They got to pay for that. When I walked in places after being cleared they kind of dropped their heads, like, "Damn, we thought we had fucked up his career, going to prison and nobody will touch him ever again." That's what they thought.

But they were wrong and that wasn't my destiny.

CHAPTER 11

Sex and drugs and R&B

Time to talk about the drugs. Weed has been part of my life since I started wearing long pants and I can't imagine a life without it. I'll smoke weed like normal people smoke cigarettes. Cocaine is an entirely different ball game.

For the first couple of years before my first album, I started snorting cocaine a little bit. You'd go to the club and you get a 20-dollar note or two 20s, and the cat behind the bar had the coke. We had friends everywhere who could supply us. So it was a club thing. You started out in the club and take a few coke lines and go do things, sing your songs and stuff like that. Gradually you begin to do more and more and more.

In the 1980s, everybody did coke. I ain't alone, it was everywhere. It was the craze in America. Everybody did coke. You'd go in the fucking offices in New York City or Los Angeles, you'd sit right in the record company's office and you'd do coke. It was no big deal. They don't give a shit about anything as long as you get the job done. You're making them money, and that's all they gave a damn about.

Flyte Tyme were the exception. They were strait-laced all the way across the board. I don't know any of them that ever smoked, drank, any of that shit – they don't do none of that.

Clarence and those guys, I was a major part of whatever they were doing and whatever they were achieving, but you can't have that drug shit around Flyte Tyme. They do not tolerate it. Rather than walk away from me, turn their back, they tried to help me, I know they did. What they didn't understand was that Alexander has always been his own man. I knew that it was important that I put out great records. That was fucking important. That was my job, to put out great records. I don't think that they came up as overbearing in my personal life. You don't agree with it, this that and the other, okay, fine. But my personal life is my business – you got to stay out of it.

I do think, at the end of our relationship, after we'd done five albums, that drugs were the reason why they didn't want to produce me anymore. But I didn't do a goddamn thing to them. I wasn't that kind of fuck up in Flyte Tyme. I wouldn't do anything to them to make them not want to be affiliated with me. Everybody over the fucking country knew that I did drugs, but I didn't care about what they say or think. I don't give a fuck about them because I don't live my life for them. Anything that's going on with this person and his life is between me and God, and me and God only.

If I ask you for your help, then you help if you want to. But you don't offer me shit because guess what? I ain't going to appreciate it and it's not welcome. It is not welcome. I am a grown man. You're a grown man. This is no accident – this is choice. I didn't get high because I had a problem. I didn't do drugs because I'm having problems. I did drugs because I goddamn wanted to, goddamn it. That's the way it was because I goddamn wanted to and it ain't nothing to do with nobody else.

Any money that I've got, I earned it. They didn't give it to me. They've had millions of dollars. I didn't have no goddamn millions of dollars. The only time I got close to a million dollars was Wembley Arena. At one point in time I had in my hand, taxes paid, money paid for, and I think I made one million dollars plus.

All those goddamn great ass songs I sang, they didn't have a problem with me singing those great songs. They didn't have a fucking problem with them going to the bank. If you don't have a problem with that, you ain't got no problem with the rest.

I wasn't disruptive in the studio. My work ethic was impeccable except for when I was getting high, when. I wouldn't go to studio because I'm not going to go there fucked up. Studio time is at nine or 10, then you change it to 11 and then 11 becomes 12 and then you call back and say I can't make it. That costs money, and it became evident that something was going on.

Truth is I'm no different to any other recording artist, from Sly Stone all the way down. Drugs don't have a damn thing to do with your performance in the studio. I don't think it helps, not that kind of drug, no – hard drugs don't help your session. Marijuana is a whole other game to me, but hard drugs, I don't think they help your session. But they don't have shit to do with the outcome of the record, they really don't. And they don't have anything to do with the outcome of your performance in a studio. They really don't because, if that's the case, then all of the great songs and albums I made, well maybe I should just take them back and scratch them off the face of the Earth. Maybe I should start over and see how I would sound clean and sober.

Clean and sober hasn't got a damn thing to do with the music industry.

People will use your drug addiction against you, especially if you are in the public eye and you're making a lot of money. They're envious. They're jealous that you could have all this opportunity, have all this money, have everything and still be a fuck up. Still be a giant fuck up, which I was, but not a fuck up to my business. That's why I kept everybody in their place with my work ethic – there wasn't anything that I'd miss. I didn't miss a bunch of shows. I didn't miss a bunch of promotions – man, I worked 16 to 18 months on the *Hearsay* album, promoting that album all over the world.

That's a lot of work and there were times when I would go back to the hotel and be exhausted. Sometimes I would work all fucking day and go to the hotel have a bite to eat, have a shower, change clothes, now I got to work all night. "I worked all fucking day now I got to go to this damn club?"

Eventually, my drug use, while not evident in the studio but through missing studio time, caused the boys in Flyte Tyme – and my accountant Byron Franks – to take action. But I resented the fact they thought they should be trying to help me. I was thinking "Who the fuck are you to try to help me? Who said I had a problem? Did I say I had a problem? Did I come to you and ask you for help? Hell no."

I agreed to go to Hazelden in Minnesota which was the best rehab centre in the country. Jimmy Jam and Terry put up the $4,000 needed for a 30-day stay.

Maybe I should have said, "No, I'll go when I want to go, I'll go do this." But I couldn't take a chance on them walking away from me because I didn't want anything to happen to my chances of getting a deal or anything to happen to my relationship with them when they were just getting started. So I went there and I completed it.

Hazelden was a fucking retreat. You ate like fucking stars, you ate the best of this and you had the best of that. It was also a bit of a sham because I didn't have one drug test the whole time

I was there. It was also pretty easy to get hold of drugs if you wanted. I stayed off cocaine while I was in there but I did have friends bring me some booze and marijuana. They would drop it off in the woods and I would walk by, spotting the package they'd left and saying, "Look what I found, Oh my God! What is that?"

Before I went into Hazelden I had decided that there's no way these motherfuckers are going to get me to sit in a chair in the middle of the floor, tell my story, start crying.

See all these motherfuckers, all these bitches, these white boys and all these brothers up in here crying, sitting up in that hot seat, telling me a story like, "And this is my last chance and, if I don't do it now, I feel like I'm going to die."

Hey motherfucker, you're going to die anyway, playboy. Check this out. I'm sitting and watching all this shit and know I'm definitely not going to have someone who is not qualified – knowledge-wise, intelligence-wise – to brainwash me. I won't do it.

I'm like, "You bitch ass motherfuckers, how dare you sit there and think you can teach me anything?"

I'm going to go through the motions.

I remember one time this counsellor sitting there and saying, "33 of you guys in here, in all probability 32 of you are not going to make it, maybe all 33." And he then said to me, "You're never going to get off drugs until you get that chip off your shoulder."

So I said to him, "All right buddy, cool, so why the fuck am I here if I ain't going to make it? See you counsellor, see you motherfucker you can't make it out there on your own, so you got to stay your ass in here coming back and counsel us. Shit, you can't function in the regular world. Everything you have to do has to be calculated. You got to have sober friends, you can't go here, you can't risk that ever. What kind of a motherfucking man are you? The only reason you ain't getting high today 'cos you up in this motherfucking place, you hanging on to this shit for dear life. Like you making a salary, doing something. You ain't doing shit for nobody. I tell you what you doing, you doing it for your own self 'cos you can't make it out there.

"Don't you sit there and tell me a motherfucking thing about me because you don't know shit about me. Don't put me in no category because you don't know shit. I don't do drugs because in my childhood I had a bad relationship with my mother, or because I didn't have a father and it scarred me, fuck that. You got the wrong ass man. I do drugs because I fucking want to. Get over it, get a life."

I remember I never saw that counsellor again – a red-haired white boy just upped and quit the job.

All the counsellors I had received the same thing from me. I'd say, "I told you, man, I got this all day every day. Look dude, you can't do shit for me. You can't tell me shit. First of all, I don't respect you. I don't respect anything you're saying. It's not welcome here. It's not going to be respected and it's not going to be received, I promise you. You can move on to the next motherfucker that you're trying to bullshit. Because you aren't shit to me. You're just some punk ass motherfucker who's up in here to save himself from drugs. You been shooting heroin all these motherfucking years, and drinking alcohol, and now you up in here turned teacher, and you think you're going to tell me something? You going to tell me anything? Man, go fuck yourself."

To be frank, there was another factor at play at that time – and that was there was no way this black man was going to have a bunch of white boys telling me shit at that point in time in my life. I thought all they had done was place obstacles in my way.

Now they were bringing up feelings inside of me, shit that I had rebelled against all my life.

Hazelden probably does work, but I'd be willing to bet you, willing to bet the farm, that it only works for five per cent, if that. Only five per cent of these motherfuckers are going home and staying clean because most of them are going right back to using drugs or back to the booze.

When I came out of Hazelden, it was 50-mile drive to my condominium. On the way home, we stopped at a drug dealer's house to buy some coke. I had my weed at home, always kept plenty of that.

CHAPTER 12

Tried to make me go to rehab

Hazelden was the first, but over the years I've been in four or five addiction centres, Betty Ford and the like, but ain't none of them ever helped me. Why? Because I never went in there for myself, always for the record company, something to do with business.

Drugs were never a problem for me. For the record companies, it was an excuse for them to fuck with me. But I was not going to let them have that, let them get away with telling the world that the problem is that I use drugs. Bullshit. You didn't say nothing the first, second, third album but now – with the fourth album – you want to start some shit.

When you are in these drug rehabilitation centres, you're supposed to be clean the whole time you're in there but, trust me, that ain't happening. A lot of them, if you're not in these clinics the whole time but allowed outside, the temptation is overwhelming to beat the system – the weekly urine test they impose to check whether you're clean.

I remember one place they gave us a certain type of piss cup with a blue top on it. After the first test, you make sure that, before the next one comes around, you'd found the same cup in a store, same distributor and everything. And you arrive for the test with this filled with tea and hidden in your pants.

You'd collect the new cup they want you to fill from the office and by the time you walk to the little testing area they've been had because the cups have been changed. No need to go out and buy a new cup for the next week 'cos the clinic's already given you one.

They test the sample, and of course, I'm clean. Looks like a duck, it walks like a duck and it quacks like a duck, but it's not a duck.

I was at my house one time chilling with some brothers when one of them told me another way to beat the test. He's sitting on the porch, and I'm looking him in the eye, he's high as a motherfucker, smoked out. I ain't saying nothing, I ain't going to judge him, I'm not going to question him, I'm not going to laugh at him or joke with him about it, I'm not going to do it. But, I know he's high as a motherfucker, he is high as a dog.

He said, "O'Neal, you want to know how I beat the piss test? Here is what you do, you get clean, dog, and then you get your jar of clean piss and put it in the fridge. You keep a jar of clean piss in the fridge so when you got to go take your piss test, boom, you got your clean sample ready to go."

Didn't like the idea too much though of keeping a jar of piss in the fridge, so for me, it was always some warm tea.

In the music scene in the late 1970s, early 1980s, cocaine was everywhere and the stars were the kings of all they surveyed.

You're in the studio, and it was a party. They had girls, they had a lot of drugs and they'd be smoking cocaine right in the fucking booth right there. It was no big deal. To them it was nothing.

If you're George Clinton, "This is what I fucking do." You're Rick James, "This is what I fucking do." You want to know why they behaved like that? Because they knew that they dominated everybody in that whole room, they were stars, that was it, cut and dried.

See, that's why I admired all these guys so much. Because, even though they got the drug stigma behind them, you can't argue with their achievements. You don't get mad at them, because they don't give a shit about what you think, or what you feel, because guess what, you're not in their presence by accident. You are allowed to be in their presence like you are allowed to be in my presence, you're allowed to be here at the studio.

If I say you got to go, you got to fucking go. Your bitch can stay, but you can go. You can send that motherfucker on the run, man, and go and check his bitch in. That's the way it was, but I never behaved like it.

For me, in the studio, I had to be on point. Especially around the guys from Flyte Tyme 'cos they were never into drugs at all. Drugs were something they didn't want a part of or have anything to do with so around them I conducted myself as such. All they know about Alex is that the motherfucker comes in the studio, he's happy, jovial, he's singing his ass off. We keep him here working until he fucking can't stand it, and then we let him go.

You can't smoke cocaine and go into the studio. I never smoked cocaine and recorded because your behaviour is too erratic. Your nervous system and everything is so off-balance because, when you're smoking cocaine, it's not the high that keeps you hooked on cocaine, it's the rush. So you have to keep smoking it to get that rush. You want to get real crazy inside, and you got to keep smoking.

As you keep smoking, they call it being sprung or being geeked. Then you get sprung and geeked where you look like a crazy person. You start behaving like a crazy person, but that's only because you went too far.

I remember one time Rick James went to Eddie Murphy's house and he was high and he jumped on his brand new couch with muddy shoes on. Eddie kicked him out. I think they said they beat Rick up or something that night, that's what they said.

They told him, "Rick, man, you went too far, man, you went too far." Rick replied, "There's no such place."

That's my boy. There's no such place. I said, "Why did you jump on Eddie's couch like that?" He said, "Because he could buy another one." I think, he did it just to show Eddie that, "I don't give a damn how big you are. I'm still Rick James, fuck you."

Outside, though, it was on, man, when I left the studio. I'd have cassette tapes of whatever we'd recorded that day and would go and see some of my girls and play them the new tracks. I'm like, "goddamn, goddamn boy. This music is to die for. It's phenomenal. These songs, what these boys are giving me, what they're giving me it's absolutely fantastic."

While I always tried to keep my shit together in the studio, things didn't always go so well on stage.

There was this one time I was due to perform in Stockholm in Sweden. I'd been doing drugs for a few days, taking Valium to come down when, just before the show, I'd sent one of the cats I was running with from London out to score me some cocaine. I wanted a few toots, a few lines, before I went on stage. He came back after a while and laid out a few lines and, thinking it was the coke he'd been sent to buy, I took a few lines. But it wasn't coke – it was heroin.

Oh God. Now, I don't do heroin. I've tried it but realized that it wasn't my cup of tea. I don't like anything about it – I hated the feeling – so, after trying it, I never did it again. This time when I snorted the heroin, everything went into a cartoon, it just happened so fast. I swear to God. I went like, "This is the best coke I ever had in my motherfucking life, man." I'm already fucked up. I'm already going down and I ain't on stage yet. I'm up all the way out of my life, man. I was behaving like a motherfucking cartoon, man.

I made it out on stage and God, it was a Nightmare on Elm Street. I'm singing songs into the mic but you can hardly hear me. Man, I sang this song, "Crying Overtime". I'm sitting on this bench, this is what everybody told me afterwards, and I start falling asleep, coming round every 10 or 20 seconds to try another line from the song, "I'll be crying". Silence. Wake up again, "Crying overtime". Back to sleep.

There must have been more than 2,000 people in the audience and all I can remember was cameras and lights flickering like it was goddamn Lee Harvey Oswald or some motherfucker.

It only ended when one of my friends came to the front of the stage 'cos he'd realized I was about to fall off. He is the one that came and got me off the stage and said, "That's it. No more. You're done."

It was horrible and I got really roasted for that. I remember people at the time saying, "Alex, I thought you were done with drugs. I thought you were this, that and the other." But I had never said a goddamn thing about being done with a motherfucking thing at that point in time. I don't know what the fuck they were talking about.

They had every right to feel whatever they wanted. But drugs were my business, not theirs. Luckily for me, we had these two old hippy guys in the crew that had travelled with us from America and they knew instantly I'd taken heroin, even though everyone knew it wasn't my drug. Them being all heroin users, they knew exactly what to do with me. They put me in a tub of cold water with ice cubes and I'd freeze my ass off. They brought me back, got me through that session and then they would ice me down again. It was all about being constantly iced down.

The next day, I looked at the newspaper and I got a big half-page picture of me with my eyes rolling around the back of my head. Every picture I saw I looked like a motherfucker that was really fucked up.

Thankfully, I flew out of Sweden the day after the concert and headed straight to London to take part in a huge charity event for Kurdish refugees at Wembley Arena. It was a massive gig with a load of superstar motherfuckers like Whitney Houston, Paul Simon, MC Hammer and Sting.

Here's me just hours earlier out of my head on heroin and next thing before nearly 13,000 people at Wembley and millions watching on television around the world. It was fantastic and I was fabulous on that show.

I remember another experience at the Apollo Theater in New York City. It's our first time out and we're having a ball. Back in the 1970s, everybody travelled with a shitload of cocaine. It was nothing to be out there and have an ounce or two of cocaine in your body. I got all my friends to come up from Minneapolis, big-time dope dealers who happened to be my friends when we grew up together. They were all excited because they were Minneapolis boys hitting New York City. They know they were with the hottest ticket going, Alexander O'Neal.

We had two shows to do and, after the first one, we had a couple of hours' free time so we celebrated with an in-dressing room party. That meant cocaine and alcohol running out of your ears.

We go out there for the second show and I'm so fucked up. I go out there and sang the same song twice. I launching into "Crying

Overtime", finished the song then, boom. "Thank you so much ladies and gentlemen. We're going to do this little song for you right now, a very pretty song. A tune called 'Crying Overtime'."

I was the band's joke for a whole week – I was the joke. They were cracking up and I didn't know what the fuck was going on. They'd be looking at me like but for days nobody had the balls to tell me shit because they didn't know how I was going to react. Eventually, I'm like, "What's going on?"

And they said, "Man, do you know that you sang 'Crying Overtime' twice in New York?"

I said, "Fuck no, I didn't. Man, you don't know the fuck you talking about."

"Yes you did Alex." Somebody else goes, "Yes you did."

That's how out of it I was.

Drugs, inevitably, got me in trouble with the law in America. Possession. It's like the old Sly Stone / George Clinton story of them in Los Angeles, riding in a Jaguar smoking cocaine. The police pulled them over. They put them in the newspaper and all that kind of shit. Okay, fine, damn. The most times I ever got busted was fucking around in a car. Stupid. I have never got busted. I've busted myself for being an idiot. That's the truth of the matter. It's always been by me having been a damn fucking idiot.

I had a cycle of every six or seven years some stupid shit would happen. Somewhere between the release of 1991's *All True Man* and 1993's *Love Makes No Sense*, I got arrested for possession of crack cocaine. Now, I've been to jail. I went to jail in Minneapolis and I never forget detectives coming down and talking to me. They were talking to me, telling me how many babies have been made to my music and all this stuff. Then they asked me, "Can you tell us something?" That means, "Give up something, give up somebody and maybe we'll let you walk." I was like, "Dawg, I ain't got nothing to say to you."

Last time I got crack busted was in 2002. I tell you, I was driving my Cadillac, I'm high as a motherfucker. It's about 8am in the morning. I'd gone to make a score. I leave the suburbs and drive to the city. Now, I ain't got no driver's licence – it's been revoked. I go and see my boy, go get some shit. But, when I get there, he says he doesn't have it fixed up like I want it fixed up, only half powder and half rock. So I took a few hits, jumped into the car and I'm flying through the city streets. I'm daring everybody and anybody – I'm defying the law and everything. I don't give a fuck about none of them, that's my attitude. I'm trying to make it to the freeway, right? Never made it. I ended up running a stop sign and there's a cop at the end of the street. It's a trap, I didn't know it, but that block there is notorious for people running the sign.

Like I said, every time I got busted it was because of my own stupidity. It wasn't because they busted me. I busted myself, because I'm an idiot. I was stupid and I acted like a drug addict. I could've tossed the drugs I had on me and all the cops would've done was towed the car and they'd let me walk home. I could've gone back later and got the drugs, right? But drug addicts don't think like that. We think we can beat everything. We can beat all the odds. So I'm thinking I can beat everything and continue home. How in the fuck could I be thinking that with no driver's licence? Goddamn, I was out of my mind. I was out of my head being high.

The cop, of course, searched the car and found some weed and coke and told me I was under arrest. There ain't no, "I don't know what that is, I ain't ever seen that before, it's not even my car." I'm going to jail and that's where I went.

Normally, I'd never spent more than a few hours inside 'cos you could normally get out on your own recognizance or through a bail bondsman.

This time, though, they kept me in all day and overnight. One thing about jail is that it's always full of different characters. And the one thing all of you have got in common is that you're incarcerated. You'll be laughing your ass off because there's always going to be something to laugh about. Somebody's telling some shit, somebody's telling some lies, somebody telling some stories. It's just like being in a comedy club.

Some of the guys locked up with me knew who I was but I didn't give a shit about that, dawg. I'd been to jail before I was a star. I didn't give a shit about that star shit, man. Jail is jail for anybody. All you need to do is be concerned about the time you get the fuck out. Well, I knew I'd get out soon as they take me to court.

When I went before the judge, I was given a three-month imposed treatment, which drove me fucking crazy. But I knew that the only way you're going to beat any bad situation you get yourself in, when it comes to the law, is that you're going to have to comply. You're not going to complete it in another way. It's not going to go away. It's only going to get worse.

At the treatment centre, you were allowed out during the day but you had to stay there overnight. Every week they would test us for drugs and every week I was clean. No weed, no nothing. I'm trying to get out of this shit. I ain't trying to fool nobody. So, I'm clean for these three months. I had to do the damn thing and I did it.

Now, when I went back to court at the end of the three months, I'm convinced I'm going to get cut loose, right? I know

I'll be on probation for two years, but I'm on my own, right? I can do anything I want, I don't have to report, no piss in no cups, I don't need to do anything. But what happens when I get there? This motherfucking counsellor says, "We think that he should stay another month. We don't think he's really ready to go yet."

I'm looking at this motherfucker like, "You what, motherfucker?" I said, "Okay, okay, okay. You want to play it like that, bitch? You want another 30 days? Okay, bitch. That's what it's going to be. But now I'm going to use my skills on you."

I was high all that fucking time. Smoked as much I could.

Every day you had to leave the centre by 8.30 in the morning and be back by six. I got high every day, I was getting blasted.

Every week when I took the urine test I beat them. They'd get me to provide a sample but, like times before, I'd give them tea instead. They're so stupid, they're not finding what they're looking for, but they're not actually looking for what this is. And what this is ain't got no cocaine in it, it ain't got no weed in it, it ain't got nothing in it.

That's just one of the tricks I used. Another game was to strap on a baby oil bottle, with the tube thing that pops out. Strap that on. They tell you to take a piss test, and they give you the cup. He's watching you riding the thing, but he's not going to watch your dick. He's watching you right through the glass. I take the cup, put it down like I'm grabbing my weenie but I'm squeezing the hidden bottle into the cup instead. Pass the test again.

This was my life. It was like this through all the days of success and even when my career started to slow down. Weed and cocaine, hand in hand. There were a lot of things I would do differently now. I would never let my children see me do drugs. In those days, if I want to do some drugs at the kitchen table, then I was going to do it. There was no privacy. Debbie was not going to challenge me on anything at that time. She had all the money, all the cars, all the clothes, she had everything.

It wasn't about the material things, but it is difficult to walk away from all that. Even though she was innocent to a lot of things, it would be difficult to walk away. Was she doing drugs? Yes, she did. She used to snort cocaine but she was not drugged out all day, every day. She would just take it occasionally. Her drug was Harmony, our daughter.

CHAPTER 13

London calling

You know there's a plan when shit happens you just can't explain. When I was a kid back in Natchez, I had this dream and it stayed with me for years.

It was a beautiful Saturday night and I was out walking the streets, but there was something weird. All over the place were these strange shaped black cabs, a style I'd never seen before. Natchez cabs were green and white.

I held on to that dream forever – it was a dream I could never translate, but it would always come back to me.

In 1986, for the first time in my life, I left the States because the first singles from my debut album had started to chart all over the world. As we pulled out of Heathrow Airport, the dream suddenly snapped into focus. London's famous black cabs were all over the place.

Of course, by that time I knew what they were. But, back in Natchez as a kid, I wouldn't have had a clue, not a chance in a million. Another sign that God had a plan for me.

My first gigs in London were in February 1986. I played the Hammersmith Odeon with Cherrelle for three nights and we sold out every single one. I didn't know there was that type of R&B enthusiasm in England even though, back in America, everybody was telling me how big I was in London, even Luther Vandross.

That first visit was a bit of an eye-opener. I was staying at the Mostyn Hotel in Marble Arch which, to me, being used to American hotels, was a bit of a dive. When we checked in I remember thinking, "Who in the hell brought me here and why am I staying in this shitty hotel?"

I was so put off by it and the people there, but I quickly discovered they were so helpful, especially the rather elderly concierge. Hell, I wasn't used to that type of kindness, it was almost like visiting your relatives house.

That concierge was a great guy and gave me a few pointers to the city. It didn't take me long on the first night to get myself out of the city and find myself a brother who could sort me out with some weed and whatever else I required.

While I've mentioned the concierge, let me tell you about a different experience elsewhere in Europe. While London has always been very welcoming to me, I cannot say the same is true for other European cities I have visited, especially Paris.

First time I went there, I didn't like it at all and my impression of the French people wasn't very good either, but perhaps I was biased coming from London. In the music industry, when you are staying in hotels and you need something or want to find your way around, all you got to do is talk to the bell boy. Basically, in America, they tend to be black. In this hotel in Paris, I got hold of the bell boy, I wasn't trying to do anything heavy, just get hold of some marijuana, some weed. This guy's looking at me as if I'm stupid, I'm talking to him and he's trying to pretend he doesn't understand me, mumbling away and shrugging his shoulders. I said, "Okay, tell you what, partner, fuck you and the horse you rode in on. I bet you understood that. Now look at me with a straight face and tell me you didn't understand what I just said to you."

My first impression of Parisians and it was as if he felt he was better than me or something just 'cos I'm black. Shit, even your bell boy at a fucking hotel. "How could you even think that, dawg? You can't even afford to stay in this hotel for one night so how could you think that?"

After that incident, I always found the Parisians I met were rude and arrogant. Every time I went to Paris after that first visit I kept my distance, and I still do so to this day. I have French relatives, in-laws, that are great and live in France and they are very kind people and very good people. It's just Paris I don't get – I don't get their attitude.

In the 1980s, when I first came to London, I would welcome most of what I encountered, but I could see, compared with the States, there were still issues.

To me, it was disappointing to see the race issues that had long divided my own country were occurring in the UK as well. The difference was that, in the States, we had challenged the system in the 1960s. In London that was only being taken up around the time I went there on tour.

Staying in hotels in central London, I just didn't get it when you saw the way black people, mostly West Indians, were treated on the streets of the West End. I did get it after a while – if they were West Indian they were going to be stopped by the police.

Walking, especially at 11pm or midnight, they are going to be stopped by the police. If they were driving a nice motor, they were almost certainly going to be stopped by the police. This was back in the day, in the mid-1980s, when it was still difficult for brothers to drive BMWs and Mercedes. You drove a BMW or Mercedes-Benz and you a black man in London, England – you getting fucking pulled-over, straight-up you getting pulled over, certainly pulled over in that motor. I don't know what that shit is all about.

I did realize that they were at least 20 years behind us in the struggle of equality because the British believe in one thing: the British society and British government. They believe in control.

Now, here's my take on such things. I don't understand a society that gives people benefits, gives grown adults benefits, to not be the best person that they could be. To me, that's the way I perceived it. I don't believe that the average person who gets benefits and get their housing paid for them should get all that for doing nothing. The whole thing in London – in Britain generally, but in London especially – is to get your rent paid. That's bullshit. That's three-quarters of the damn battle right there. That's three-quarters of the life battle getting your rent paid. London, I would say, is one of the three most expensive cities in the world to live in, if not the most expensive. Most of London society is battling to be able to afford their rent, and they depend on benefits. To me, I see that as a way of controlling people, because receiving benefits makes you dependent upon the government. When that happens, they start to depend on benefits like they depend on breathing air.

Some of them will try to make their life a little better along with the benefits. But here's my point about that, which is very simple. When you take a grown-ass healthy man that should be out taking care of himself and his family, working for it, and he's getting benefits – that's not right. It's not right because what you do is you take all of his self-worth away from him. If they have any type of desire to be anything in life, you take that away.

When you get dependent upon the government, upon benefits and things like that for your lifestyle, that's not good. You're an adult. You're supposed to be working and paying. It's not supposed to be three quarters of the country who get the benefits and the other quarter who pays for it all. That's not the way this shit's supposed to go. Even the Bible said that man is supposed to prosper by the sweat of his own brow. That means you work for your shit.

Shit, I wouldn't mind if somebody paid my rent. That wouldn't hurt me at all. But guess what? I have to pay for myself and I'm always used to paying my rent. Back in the 1970s in the States we changed our welfare system tremendously but I never agreed with it. We have this program called General Assistance where you could come in from another state, almost like a refugee, and get benefits.

What they don't realize is that, every time you take those benefits, you become a professional welfare or benefit person. You've just lost so much valuable time in your life that you should be applying to your own success, your own prosperity. You can't even pursue your dream because you're so damn worried about making sure that you get your benefits straight.

Your future has been taken away from you because all you can do is toe the line because you got to get your benefits. If they don't pay it then how's it going to paid? You sure can't pay it. Why can't you pay it? You know why you can't pay it? Because you're not man enough. You're not man enough to pay it. That's exactly what it comes down to. You're not man enough to pay it, you can't pay it and that means you can't keep a roof over your head because you just can't take care of yourself because you're used to somebody taking care of you. You're a grown ass man.

Now, there are those programs that are designed for people who really need them. And, for those people, I have no beef at all. Whether you're male or female, young or old, black, white or blue – it doesn't matter. If you need help, you should get help. But not permanently. Not your whole young adult life.

"I got benefits when I was 25 years old and I'm now 55 and

I'm still getting benefits." That should not be. They have just taken your whole fucking life away from you. That's my take on that. I have never agreed with the concept of controlling people.

This is stuff I've learned through life. Of course, in the early days of my stardom, this sort of shit wasn't in my mind, I was tripping out on life and didn't think much about anything.

In Britain, the racism is still there, not as blatant as when I first came here in the 1980s, but it's there all right. Having said that, I have only been called a nigger on two occasions in London and both times it was by people who were drunk.

The first was in Swiss Cottage just a few years ago when I'd just gone to use a cash machine. As I walked away there were two white boys and one of the said, "Hey nigga." Hey, nigga! When I heard that word, wow. If this had happened when I was younger, I'd have gone straight over and jacked his ass. Now though I'm a grown man and I don't want that. I'm a responsible man, and I don't have to respond to ignorance with another piece of ignorance because that's not going to solve anything.

The other time it happened was in Kilburn and these guys are drunk too. I'm like, "You know what, dawg, fuck with that, I'm not going to fuck with you, because I heard you, and you drunk, and now you got your instant courage, and I'm your joke right now, so you want to say something stupid. I'm going to let that go – I'm going to be bigger and better than that."

Sometimes I get sick of being bigger and better. Some people certainly deserve to get their damn teeth knocked down their fucking throats. But, if you do that, you're wrong. It's a no-win situation. I'm going to try to steer clear of all that shit and I'm going to try to advocate for loving one another and taking care of one another.

I'd come back to London again in December 1989 for what became – for an R&B artist – a record sell-out six nights at Wembley Arena.

When we arrived in England, we're tripping on money. That was a surprise to me, as much money as I'd made back in the States. But that's still nothing in comparison with what the white acts make. Wembley, it was a huge thing, but I wasn't thinking about the hugeness. I wasn't thinking about any of that. When I came to London, it was a time in my career when I thought it'd always be like that. When I went back to America, I went back with a million plus for six nights of my time.

In 1989 for a brother to have that much love in London, in England, to sell out six nights at Wembley Arena. That's love.

Headlining a huge, 12,000-seater like Wembley Arena was a great accomplishment – the height of my career. It was a Paul Revere moment, a shot heard around the world.

For arranging Wembley, we'd used our promoter Byron Orme's BKO Productions who would announce one date and it would sell out, agree to do another show and that would sell out until in the end, we had signed up for six nights in a row. It's a record, I think, which still stands today.

Before I got to London, though, I had problems with the band I had put together for the show. One of the guys, Noah Hickman, told me there was a mutiny going on over how much the band should be paid for the London shows. We were due to fly out in just two days, so I really didn't need this grief. I approached the guy who had raised the problem, the drummer, and said, "So how much do you think you should be getting paid per show?" The band would have been on about $200 each a night and he wanted a raise and asked for $250.

I told him, "Your price is fine, the band will get it but you sure as hell won't be fucking getting it from me, you mutinous motherfucking snake in the grass. You can go to hell."

I fired his ass and paid the rest of the band an extra $100 a night just to shut them down.

At that time, you – the artist – paid your musicians a set fee irrespective of the size of the gig and how much is being made. All those profits are my profits, not yours. You are here to do a job, do a service. Your job is to go and play per night, be patient, get on stage and play the show. That's your job. You knew what the deal was and you agreed to it when I hired you. You knew what the job was paying.

In addition to the band, I'd also hired a dancer to appear with us in London, Cynthia. She'd just got back to Minneapolis after living out in California and, when she turned up at the audition, she had all this West Coast pizzazz going on. My first impression was that she was stunning, absolutely gorgeous. Unlike other petite, skinny dancers she looked strong, more heavy set. I was thinking, wow, that's my kind of girl. She danced for a few seconds and I said, "Okay, fine, you got the job." Little did I know how things were going to pan out between us.

When we got to Wembley, the first couple of shows were fantastic. It was laid out, it was a big show, big production, two hours plus which was unheard of. The press were all writing about it. By the third night, however, I knew there was a problem, I could feel my voice was going and on that third night it went out. I'd just burned myself out staying up all the time doing my shit, not getting proper rest, taking naps. Going to the show, I could feel I was not right but I thought I was young and could cope, so I thought "no big deal".

A key part of the show was a scene where I'd invite a girl up from the audience and sit her on a bed on stage while serenading her. I'd change into a smoking jacket and give her a bouquet of roses. That night I'd cut this to try and save my voice but it wasn't enough and I had to end the performance early. When I lost my voice, all hell broke loose in the arena. People wanted their money back and all kinds of shit.

Next day it was all over the papers, "Alexander O'Neal bombs out at Wembley."

I went to see a good friend of mine at Capital Radio, the DJ John Sachs, and he told me just to get some rest, give it 24 hours to see if the voice came back. To be honest, I was scared 'cos this was a big scene with a lot of money riding on it. Thankfully Rocky Garrity, the bass player in the band, told me what to do. He said, "This is how you get your voice back. Get some rest, drink water, lots of water until it's running out of your ears."

I drank water all that day, all night, all the next day. When I got ready to go to the show the next night I had my voice back and I was so pleased.

That Saturday night I'd agreed for the show to be videoed. I'd be paid an extra $250,000 for a VHS release entitled *Alexander O'Neal Live at Wembley*. When I went on stage I was still tired as a motherfucker but determined to put on the best show I could, and I put my heart and soul into it. In my heart I knew that, if the video had been shot on the first or second nights of the Wembley run, it would have turned out better because those performances were red hot. Still, I gave it all I could and it came out all right, but it was a hard night.

The loss of my voice wasn't the only problem in London as I mentioned earlier. Debbie had fucked me over.

Debbie and the girls had come on the trip and I'd arranged for them to stay in a suite at the Holiday Inn. I had my own suite there as well which only my daughter Alexandra would come into. Harmony and Debbie just left me alone. I also had a suite at the Ritz-Carlton where I could chill out, take my weed and cocaine and stuff.

By the end of the Wembley shows, I had just over a million dollars in the bank, the most money I'd ever earned in one go.

I was on a high but it was on the flight home when I discovered that Debbie and Byron Orme had met with the guys I'd hired out of Chicago to set up the London gigs and they'd persuaded her to sign over $50,000 to them. In total these guys, Clinton and Andrew, walked away with $135,000 when I was only supposed to pay them $50,000 in total.

I was devastated that Debbie had done this. To this day she has never explained why she did it. What had they said to get her to sign over the money? Did they say that I was getting ready to leave her for Janet, my road manager? Probably. That's very probably what they said. That's just me thinking of possibilities of what could have happened.

That was the beginning of the end right there for her. From that point on I set about being the most dominant brother I could be, making her life absolutely holy hell. I was going to keep her in a subservient place where she could never get out. And she was never going to come out, as far as I was concerned. In my book, she never was going to get out of that, ever.

That's a bad time, a really bad time, and very sad.

CHAPTER 14

Jimmy Jam and Terry Lewis

After the success of the first two albums and the massive single hits with "Criticize" and "Fake" in 1987, we were determined to keep the whole thing rolling.

A lot of times artists get a record deal and they're lucky if their first album is even noticed. What we'd been doing had got the whole world paying attention.

Jimmy Jam and Terry were very supportive 'cos they were now stars in their own right, producing and writing such great material. Often the producers are very much in the background, but not these guys. They wanted to be stars, and they used everything that they could in a positive way to get there. They appeared in my first album, they appeared in my video, they made themselves stars. They had their own pedigree, they wore the shades and the glasses. It was like they were the black Blues Brothers. When you saw them, you knew instantly who they were.

For our third album, we decided to produce something specifically for the Christmas market. Nobody was doing that until Alexander O'Neal. The album just dominated the airwaves during the holiday season. That album, *My Gift To You* was a really good album, a mix of Jimmy Jam and Terry Lewis originals and old Christmas songs like "Little Drummer Boy" and "Winter Wonderland". Of course, why wouldn't it be good, given all the great guys involved? We weren't just chasing the money. We just wanted to put a stamp down on our music.

We gave ourselves two weeks to complete, which Clarence Avant said couldn't be done. Man, if you're willing to do the work you can do anything. We went into the studio and we crammed. We did a couple of songs a day, they were mixing it as we were recording it and the album cover was shot when we got a break from the studio.

1991's *All True Man*, my fourth album, was another hit. Working with the guys again, we were doing stuff that was way ahead of our time. We did *All True Man* backwards because what we did was we found there were things that I wanted to talk about and wrote songs around those subjects. I had never done a session where we recorded the vocals and then they put the music to the vocals after that. It was always the music and then the vocals, so that was some different shit for me but it was beautiful and it worked. It was a good time.

Because Terry and Jimmy were really in demand, I had to wait about 16 months in-between albums before we could get in the studio again together. I could have put an album out earlier, but I wouldn't have them as producers. Other people approached me with separate deals behind Clarence and Tabu's backs but my loyalty was to them. I could have gone to Bridge Records and probably made a shitload of money but would I have had the same type of success in my career? Would I have the same type of foundation? I wasn't willing to walk away from Flyte Time to find out. Also, other producers may have thought that they could create that Minneapolis/Flyte Tyme sound, but I was never convinced. I was going to wait for the real deal, Jimmy Jam and Terry. That is the big league, that's where big boys roam. That's where the big record and distribution companies live. You walk in with a Jimmy Jam and Terry Lewis song any motherfucker up there, every company is going to want to buy it.

At that time I was very happy with the situation, even though the albums seemed slow coming out. Looking back now what we achieved is embedded in history. You can't say "Minneapolis music scene" without thinking Alexander O'Neal and that's crazy, dawg.

We had something that was so good, and it was a match made in Heaven. The respect Jimmy and Terry showed me as an artist was phenomenal. But at the same time I knew that they had different feelings for Alex the person and Alex the artist.

That always had been the case because I lived very differently to the way they lived. I'm not the people they are, that's not my lifestyle at all, but everybody got a closet and everybody got something in it.

Deep down I've always felt that they didn't respect me as a person. They certainly respected my talent, and they showed respect towards my personal life because they never got involved there. But I always felt that maybe some of them around Flyte Tyme, not all of them but some of them, felt they were better than me. My talent was better than all that bullshit, because there's no such thing as better than anybody. Nobody is better than anybody else.

Every time I did something successful my whole persona went up a notch. Everything was escalating like it was getting ready to peak out. With *My Gift To You* and *All True Man* both successes, I've now got even more money coming in on top of the stuff I'm getting through tours and stuff.

I'm making more money and more money and more money. Actually, at that time I was living the life. I was living high on the hog and didn't have any worries. Nobody ever told me that this would ever end. I thought, this is the way it was going to be. I thought that I could make these decisions, these choices, for my whole life, my whole career. But I was really new to this stardom game. I was in for a rude awakening, to find out that no, this is not the way it is and it's not automatic and you don't have all this prosperity all the time. You got some up times, you got some down times and you got things in life that you got to deal with.

I should have kept my private life over here, the business over there, and this over here. They all just went together because I was just high on the hog at that time.

I'd be smoking cocaine or snorting it all the time. Success didn't do nothing but stabilize my drug abuse. The more money, the more drugs. The more money, the more I didn't have to worry about drugs.

I never looked at myself as a junkie or a crackhead, as they would call me. Because I smoked cocaine so, therefore, I guess I would be considered a crackhead. Let them say it, but that's the nastiest term. When they use the word crackhead, that's designed to hurt you, to hurt your spirit, to hurt your heart. It's a name to put their foot on your back and keep it there, and they want you to stay down. That word crackhead means that you ain't shit, it means that I don't give a damn how good you are, what good you do for people, how kind you are to them, whatever. They don't even see the times that you're not even high. They don't see those times.

If you're around them and you're not even high, they won't give you that. If you bring something good to their life, they won't give you that either but they'll give you the title, when they're angry at you or upset or you have a row or a problem, guess what you are? A crackhead, motherfucker.

The only reason those people use those terms are because they are fucking losers and wannabes. I'd much rather be a "has been" than a "never was". Those motherfuckers who use terms like crackhead ain't nothing. They ain't never going to be shit. I said it and I meant it.

Sitting around, being miserable, trying to put down everybody else's life, put down the shortcomings in their own life – it's about them. They're the ones who can't do it.

Drug addicts are not supposed to be able to do what I've been able to do. They're not supposed to be able to achieve what I've achieved. If you're a drug addict, you're supposed to use all your money, all your assets, on drugs. And, when you have no more success in your career, then you're supposed to be a has-been drug addict and nothing more. Someone who went down, someone who let crack and cocaine take him out of the industry.

Now, I don't care how many drugs I fucking used – I still went to work. In the beginning, I used to go on stage and I'd be high. Shit, I'd take a blast right in the dressing room. I stopped doing that very shortly after the *Hearsay* album.

I stopped because Noah Hickman, he just sat me down one day and said about being true to one thing. You've got to find out what that one thing is. The one thing for me happened to be music. My true thing was what I do on stage.

I recognized that people who had read about my use of cocaine would be thinking that they were taking a chance on coming to see me in concert. Would I show up, or would I decide that I couldn't be bothered? That's what drug addicts do. They decide that afternoon that they will be getting high all day and all night long. They decide that they're not going to go on, then they don't go. They cancel the show.

But I never cancelled a goddamn show in my whole life. I've always gone to my job. I always took care of it.

By the time of my fourth album, *All True Man*, in 1991, I'd been sent by record companies to a number of clinics and I had now had enough. It was apparent that some of the boys surrounding Flyte Tyme had turned against me. I was sick of motherfuckers in my life trying to tell me what to sort out. They don't get that opportunity any more. I'm done with that. I don't want to hear anything that they've got to say. They know I don't want to hear it.

If it was going to lead to a parting of the ways, then I was prepared. I was doing a great job here and if those motherfuckers wanted to use my drug use to say, "I don't want to work with you, I don't want to deal with you," then go on and do what you need to do. I was doing drugs from the goddamn first album. I did drugs on every damn album.

You didn't have a fucking problem going to the bank, and you didn't have a problem cashing millions of dollars. You do whatever you want to do, and obviously they did. Now all of a sudden I'm a problem. I wasn't a problem to no Flyte Tyme production because of my drug use. If anybody said that's the biggest pack of bullshit I've ever heard all my life.

I wasn't no problem to Tabu records through my drugs. I only became a problem when they didn't want to deal with me, when they didn't want to be affiliated with me anymore. Because I was too opinionated, nobody could tell me what to do. I guess they used the term "hot-headed". They couldn't accept that I didn't want to be like them. I didn't want to be clean.

I did drugs at the time because I got high, because I like getting high. I liked doing it. I have no excuse. I didn't decide to get high because I was feeling bad. I got high because I wanted to.

They knew I didn't have to explain myself. As long I come in here and I release great ass albums, it doesn't matter.

My work ethic has always been damn good, so you can't have no beef with me. Nobody was forcing me to do all these interviews and nobody was making me get up and do all these promotional tours, all over the country. I did it because I knew it had to be done. It was a part of the damn deal.

If I'm so fucked up and so bad, how the fuck could I do all that? All of this shit that they were getting was second-hand news and shit like that. They were getting the wrong information.

I just let them go on because I'm not going to sit up and try to explain myself and my drug addiction to anyone at that point.

To be clear, I never felt let down by Clarence Avant and my Flyte Tyme brothers. Clarence has only been there every way that he could. Anything that I wanted to achieve, he's been there. Clarence has a paternal relationship with me. I know I feel that way about him and I feel like he feels the same way about me. He's a friend but it's also a father-son kind of thing. I always gravitate to any man who is paternal to me because that's a father that I never had. The respect level that I have for him and the loyalty has been phenomenal.

If I'm not a multi-millionaire right now, it's not the fault of Clarence nor anybody else. It's my own fault. I've had enough money and enough chances and enough success.

I'm not going to look back and say, "These guys got all this success and I have nothing." Well, if I have nothing, it's because I didn't do anything significant with the money I earned. I lived like every night was Saturday night. That was my philosophy, that's the way I lived and I enjoyed it. I had a ball.

I had a ball, but I was always very conscious of what the

fuck I was saying and what I was doing. Clarence Avant has been there for me every step of the way. He's been very supportive in everything I've been doing. He would have shown me the game if I had asked him. He would have shown me how to take my money and how to make my money work and how to really do things. Why didn't I ever ask? Because I don't have the same dream as Jimmy Jam and Terry Lewis, I don't have the same dreams as Cherrelle, I don't have the same dreams as a lot of people. I'm saying that my dreams are not as big as their dreams are.

I don't want them to be, not because I'm a small-minded person, but because I choose to not to have those type of ambitions. In my head I don't want, "You gotta want to be a millionaire, you gotta want a big house and Ferraris and all that millionaire shit." You gotta want that and I don't want that. That's not something that I set out to achieve.

By 1993, the way things were around Tabu and Flyte Tyme, I was ready to do my first album with other producers.

The main guys working with me were and Prof T. I was cool working with them because I knew we'd get a great album, which we did. The title song "Love Makes No Sense" was a Top 20 hit in the UK, but it should have been an anthem like "Fake". The new song was as good as any of that shit and maybe even better.

The problem we encountered was that the distributors A&M shut down their R&B division. With that the album didn't get any real support from the record company.

It was released and half-ass supported. Maybe it's because Jimmy Jam and Terry didn't write the songs. But we certainly didn't get the same love, even though we were the same company, with the same people.

Whoever was supposed to be doing the publicity on *Love Makes No Sense* really dropped the ball. I don't know if it was deliberate or accidental, I don't give a fuck. I do know one thing for sure, that somebody dropped the ball on that album.

I knew in my heart that the record company were now just shipping me out the back door.

CHAPTER 15
Motown

Clarence Avant always stood by me, and it was his actions that brought about my final break with Terry, Jimmy Jam and the boys. Clarence was a big hitter in the music industry and, seeing his success with Tabu Records, it was no surprise to see him being asked to take over at Motown. He took me with him.

Unfortunately, Motown was a horrible experience for me. I was still signed to Clarence and they had me for a year but didn't put out an album. They'd decided they did not want to fuck with me because of my drug use and every damn thing else.

I like drugs, and the label could not turn their eye away from the fact that I did not give two fucks about them. My position was that they should be focusing on my achievements. Instead, everybody wanted to deal with me on my personal issues, and that was drugs. That is all they ever wanted to say about me.

I'd go out and tear shows up, turn the shit up. When I got back, they'd say, "I heard you had a great show in New York. I heard you had a great show in Philadelphia." No, what they really wanted to tell me was they'd heard that I scored some drugs in Philly, because they'd have people monitoring this shit. They had guys taking any information that anyone was willing to give them.

Motown can kiss my ass. I got no respect from them. They've got their big-time artists out there, right. But, when I joined, the rest of their artists were a roster full of nobodies.

I was working with Zack Harmon and Chris Troy who were like their Jimmy Jam and Terry Lewis. They'd written with me on

Love Makes No Sense but the Motown sons of a bitches said that every song we came up with was not even good enough to put out. I heard releases of these songs later on in my career but they apparently they were not good enough for my album.

It was not that the music was not good enough – they did not want to put an album out, period. They did not want to put any real effort into Alexander O'Neal. A black label turning their back on a black man? Believe that shit. Now how can we afford to do that to each other? It was just like when Motown turned their back on Marvin Gaye after all the damn shit he'd done for them. Remember I said, unlike the white folks, we don't take care of each other. There you see it. That is what we do as black people. Once again, it's very nasty. We do not take care of each other. We would rather destroy each other than take care of each other. And that is atrocious. This is the truth of the matter – it is not a lie.

Motown was the worst situation I have ever been in during my life. My shit from that time is still sitting on a shelf in Motown. I couldn't even finish a damn album before they decided they do not even want to fuck with me. However bad the situation was though I had to stick with it because I was in a bad place at this point in time. I didn't have the money I had before. I'm poor. I'm broke. Motown is giving me $8,000 a month but, except for $250, I was sending it all back to Debbie and the girls who were now living in Las Vegas.

I'm in Los Angeles trying to record an album. I'm living in a hotel on $250 a week – an amount that I can barely feed myself on – and I have a drug habit that is enormous.

Being broke is a motherfucking joke up in Hollywood. If I didn't know my way around and didn't have friends in Los Angeles, I'd have been up shit creek. My very good friend Sue

Ann Carwell was a great singer from Minneapolis who had hooked up a deal with Warner Brothers. She had moved out to LA and she saved my ass. She took me to all the good people she knew, people like Penny Ford. Penny was a great artist but another who didn't get the love she deserved. All these people were my friends and they were mostly women. There was no pimping, there was no hustling, there was nothing, it was a paid up "I love you, Alex," "I love you, Sue Ann."

She took care of me. She took care of me like fucking gold when I was in LA, got me through this motherfucking situation when I was broke as a fucking joke. I didn't have no money, and the drug addiction was up so high that I couldn't even fucking cross the damn street. How is $250 a week going to support that? It was a nasty situation. It was a nasty time for me in LA, nasty.

I was going to the studio three or four times a week trying to do the album. But, as good as I knew I was, my spirit was so low. I couldn't have gotten the best of me even if I'd have tried. I was pushing myself to another level, trying to be the best, trying to have that same drive that I had doing my other albums but I didn't have it.

Why? Because I wasn't living. I didn't have the comfort level. I had no comfort at all and that was a bad.

On top of everything, I'm sending the money back to Debbie in Vegas and I'm feeling some funny shit is going on. I'm in LA. I'm doing all this shit to keep the $8,000 coming in to my family every month. At that time I knew I didn't have $8,000 worth of bills, so how the fuck would $8,000 a month be gone? I guessed that it was going somewhere between her and the secret lover that I suspected she had.

Motown tightened the noose when they cut the monthly salary to $6,000.

They're still holding on but they are getting ready to let me go. They're paying me $6,000 a month not to record, $6,000 a month not to do a damn thing until they decide to drop me. That's the way it really came out, because they never had a plan.

They were appeasing Clarence Avant for a while. And, once they got tired of him, they just said, "No, we are going to drop Alex, period."

After paying me for a year, they just washed their hands of me.

Now, at this point, my career is supposed to be over. Yet here I am, 20 something years later, and I'm still going. I'm still recording albums. You don't stop doing what you do just because something is not successful, you keep going.

I was back in Vegas after the Motown thing had ended and now life was about to throw another curveball at me. It was at this point that Debbie decided to call time on our marriage.

I don't know if there was a final straw, as dominant as I was, she never talked to me to give me an ultimatum to change.

Debbie walked out when my career had stalled. The shit was going downhill, the drugs had taken us downhill financially. She was putting all my business out on the street, getting therapy from the motherfuckers out there. I stop people if they start talking to me about something which is irrelevant to me, something about other people. Whatever differences you have with someone else, whatever problems they have if you want to tell me, I don't want to hear it.

These were the last days for Debbie and me. We were living in a $2,000 apartment in Las Vegas and I couldn't even keep the lights on. We were bootlegging electricity from an outlet in the complex. I had no money, it was bad and I didn't even know how to feed my kids. I had nothing.

On top of all this, I still needed the drugs. Here my cousin Alexander Shaw, who lived in Vegas, helped out. He made sure that dealers knew I was good for the money, even if it took a bit of time to get it. Alex was a lifesaver for me and he also kept me going mentally. My Las Vegas family, my people, didn't turn their backs on me. They stayed in there with me. I had a line of credit, okay? I had drug dealers around me. They were all family. They knew I was going to get money. My account went up to $3,500 and I paid it all. If you don't pay these motherfuckers, that's the kind of shit that gets you killed.

So now I could get my drugs plus I've been using everything I could, pawning every damn thing I could and borrowing money from across the country. Most of it was from my family, my sisters, my mother. Those were the ones who were helping me with $100 here and $100 there. That meant a lot to me.

Eventually, I got a gig in Germany which got me back on my feet. I flew back into the States with $30,000 and immediately cleared my debt with the dealers.

The day Debbie left I got a call from the girls' school saying she hadn't turned up to pick our daughters up. It was almost five in the afternoon when I managed to get down there and picked them up. I rang Debbie on her phone and she sounded high and I guessed she was with someone. A couple of days later, she vanished taking the girls with her. I didn't see or hear from them for four fucking years.

Turned out I was right with that feeling I had back in LA that something wasn't right – she was seeing another guy, a married man. He's her knight in shining armour I guess. He's saved Debbie from Alexander O'Neal, the abusive drug addict. Later I got a message to him: "Your claim to fame, punk bitch ass motherfucker, is getting Alexander O'Neal's ex-wife. You come in here like you saving her, but you're just a parasite motherfucker. You coming in and you think you got something, but you ain't got shit. And listen, she's going to do the same thing to you. She's a runner."

When Debbie paid me back for all the shit that I did, she didn't pay in instalments – she paid in full. She broke my motherfucking heart off the Richter scale. She broke it so nasty that everything I had feared about her, that's exactly what the fuck she was doing. She had surrounded herself with a bunch of scum-ass, no-good niggers. I would never allow her or my daughters to be around those kind of people, but I guess they convinced her that I was scum.

Debbie knew there was one thing that would make certain of her and me never being together again and that was her being with another man. She knew that if I was to even hear word that she's with another man, then I would never want her again. I didn't give a fuck what I did but she knew that, in order to really make it game over, the move she'd made did that. She's not coming back because I didn't want her back. It was truly over.

Her nightmare was over. Me being at her, being abusive verbally, physically. All of that shit. My drug habit and all of the things that came along with that, like her making all of those drug runs for me. All of that shit was over. All she'd needed to do was have an affair. Because, once another man has touched something that's supposed to be mine, that means it's not mine anymore. You can have that. We couldn't have gotten back together. There's no happy ending for that situation, in any situation, not with Alexander O'Neal.

That's fine. Debbie walked away but, as it turned out, she jumped right out of the skillet into the frying pan 'cos he whipped her ass. Now she was going through the same shit with a poor-ass motherfucker who ain't got shit. Some saviour.

Okay, she was gone, I realized she had to do what she had to do for her own survival, and at that time shit, if I was her, I'd have done the same thing. But you mean to tell me that she's not letting me see my daughters for four years? You don't think she knew that those girls were my heart and soul? She knew that they were my everything and that it would break my heart to not see or hear from them for so long.

To this day, as much as I accept my part in the break-up of that marriage, it still haunts me, it still comes back. Because I never thought it would be over for good, I thought that it would be her and me for life. But I never got a chance. The thing that probably messes with my head the most is that I never got a chance to get it right. I never even got a chance to talk.

For the next four years, I am constantly looking for these motherfuckers. I don't want him, and I don't give a fuck about him. I just want my daughters, my princesses who I treated like gold.

They were Debbie's best friends. That's how she survived me. I can see that now. But to sit down and to think that, as much as I loved those girls, I didn't deserve one fucking phone call for four years.

When Debbie walked out, I discovered things I'd thought she was looking after hadn't been taken care of and I hadn't seen that coming. When I was in LA, she'd rung and asked if we could buy an apartment. I'm like, "Okay, cool no problem," but only to find out now there was like $18,000 worth of fucking mortgage due. I never knew about all this shit. I never knew about the business stuff, I just sent her the money and lived my own life thinking that she was taking care of business. She sure was taking care of business – her business. She wasn't taking care of our business.

I was stupid because, once again, I was leading with my heart, not my head. I had to sell the house. Fuck, I got stiffed on that deal. I lost $33,000. I had all this stuff in storage back in Minneapolis – pianos, motorcycles, all kinds of shit worth a goddamn fortune. She hadn't paid a bill for more than a year and we were like $20,000 in arrears. They gave me an ultimatum to pay but, shit, I didn't have the money at that time. So all that shit was lost.

At this time one of the things I had to hold on to was Cynthia, who was back in Minneapolis. Cynthia was one of my dancers during the shows at Wembley Arena and was very dear to me. Debbie knew this and had asked me to stop seeing her which I had refused. There was no way in hell that I was going to give up a good woman like Cynthia.

Another weird thing around this time, before Debbie vanished, was at drug bust during a visit to Minneapolis. As a result, I'd been placed on an outpatient scheme at the Excelsior Project in the city and I needed to stay with someone during the four months of treatment. Debbie allowed me to live with Cynthia the whole time. Things were going okay between me and Debbie all through this, because Cynthia is just not her business. But I think it is awfully strange for a woman to let her husband live with his mistress openly and still come back home. That's weird.

Of course, the reason why was because she was seeing someone else herself.

Ever since then I'd known it was only a matter of time before Debbie left me for good. I just didn't know the manner in which she'd do it.

I'm sure, in Debbie's mind, she thought I would be running after her, so angry that she'd left with the kids that I would be mad enough to even kill her. Debbie was running for years, thinking she was going to look over her shoulder and I was going to be there to cut her damn head off or OJ Simpson her ass.

She was wrong. She was wrong because what she didn't know is that you can run all you want, but at some point you will turn around and you'll see that there is nobody chasing you. You're just running. Because you're running from your own guilt, your own shame, because you didn't have the balls to even tell me that you're leaving.

You didn't have the balls enough to say, "Alex, I'm going to leave you and it's going to be for good." Debbie, you didn't do that. You hurt me in the biggest way you could.

I did spend months looking for the girls 'cos I still wanted them in my life, but not their mother.

Eventually, I knew I was in a rut and said to myself, "I'm going have to do something about this. I need to get up, Vegas is over, okay. I got to get out of Vegas, it's done. There's no reason for me to be here. If I can't find my children, I can't find them. She's in Vegas, but I can't find them. I've got shit happening. This is over. You've got to move on."

It's going to come back around 'cos you're never going to lose your kids for life. It's going to come back around. But I decided that this part of my life was over. It's happened to you Alex. Now, how are you going to deal with this, man?

The answer was to stay working, use all my contacts and tighten up my shit.

I decided that I was going to go back to Minneapolis. Together with Cynthia, I am going to start my life again. And that's what I did. Cynthia and I have been together now for 27 years.

CHAPTER 16
Back in Minneapolis

When I left Vegas to go back to Minneapolis, the only thing I took was my Corvette. Everything else I just left in the apartment and walked away. It was a two-day drive back to the Twin Cities and, as soon as I arrived, I moved in with Cynthia, who had her own place. She was my woman, a great woman, and she was my world. She was going to take care of business and make sure that my shit was taken care of. The only thing I needed to worry about is getting myself back up. I had to get my shit together and figure out which way I am going.

I knew Terry Lewis and Jimmy Jam were having success with their own record company, Perspective Records, but at this time pretty much felt abandoned by them and all the boys from Flyte Tyme.

That's when God intervened again 'cos, out of the blue, Terry's on the phone asking me to sign to their label. When somebody wants to do something for me, it's always Terry.

They're offering me $50,000 front money to sign. I was like, "Damn, dawg, you know I'm up to like 250."

When I was with Tabu and Motown, I'd be getting something between 250 and 500 thousand dollars for an album. I knew Perspective was not a major label, but the offer was very low. It was like they were saying that I'm broke and I've got to take this. Like, "You don't have shit, you don't have a record out there, you don't have nothing, nigga, you've got to be glad that we've offered you this deal."

I'm not saying that this was the truth behind their offer, but that's how it felt to me. I felt that $50,000 was insulting to me. I felt he should have offered $100,000 at least to give me something to motivate me.

What Terry didn't know is that I did have a couple of other offers on the table besides Perspective's. One was from One World Records, which was run by a good friend of mine from New York, Buzz Willis, and another guy, Alan.

I was at the point in time in my career that virtually everybody had already turned their back on me. But now I've got an offer from Perspective on the table for $50,000, and I've got an offer with Buzz for $100,000. Which one am I going to go with? It had to be a business decision, so I went with Buzz. The added attraction was I would be in charge, unlike with Terry and Jimmy Jam, and also working with two great producers out of England, Dennis Charles and Ronnie Wilson, who'd had great success with the band Eternal.

I'll always be grateful to Buzz for his friendship and for sticking by me. Buzz Willis helped me when I couldn't help myself, when I was down, Buzz was right there for me. He put me back on deck when he could have turned his back like everybody else.

I remember one incredible thing he did for me one time when I was staying overnight in a hotel in New York before catching a flight to the UK. Of course, the first thing I'd done is go down the street and got some shit to smoke in the room. In New York I knew where to go to get the drugs, I knew exactly where to get the shit. I'm getting high when Buzz rings up and tells me he's sending my hero, Kool Bell – of Kool & The Gang – to come over and chill with me. Him and Kool Bell were like brothers.

He comes over and he really is cool. He's a good brother. For an hour or so we kicked it, talked and stuff like that. I'm in awe because this is Kool Bell, this is Kool & The Gang. We're both big stars, but I'm still honoured to be with him. Once we get on, one black man to another, it's all good – although all the time I'm trying to maintain my coolness because I've just been getting high. I can't take no hits in front of Kool. I can't do no shit in front of Kool. I'm trying to be hospitable, I'm trying to keep calm and keep my insides inside. It feels like my guts are about to come out. I want to go and take a bucket of blast. But I'm still in awe of Kool, and it got me through.

I think Buzz sent Kool over as a positive rock, something for me to hang on to. He's someone that doesn't get high and never has. That's the only encounter I've ever had with Kool Bell but he felt, on that night, like somebody I could trust.

While Buzz was a great friend, everything didn't go as well as I hoped with One World Entertainment. The company was a subsidiary of one of the major labels and dealing with them wasn't easy.

On signing they'd given me $50,000 upfront but getting the rest turned into a nightmare. We got the album *Lovers Again* done but there was some power thing between One World and the parent company and they just skated around, dragging their feet on paying the rest of the money that was owed. It took ages with a load of jargon to hold me off. I'd get $10,000 here, $20,000 there, and the whole thing just pissed me off.

At one point while we were recording, the album had been all over the place. I had my good friend Nick Mundy come in to give it some stability. Nick is a producer who I got into my family from Sue Ann Carwell, my girl in California.

At the end of our time in the studio, I was pleased with a lot of the material. But I wasn't happy with the one thing I'd asked them not to do – and that was to get the album mastered in England. This is because England does not know how to master R&B music. They don't have a clue.

We had agreed that they would take it to Bernie Gunman in Los Angeles. Bernie has always mastered all my albums, and it's fine with Bernie. No, at the end of the day when the album was ready, after we'd recorded all the songs and everything, they went and mastered it at Abbey Road.

I guess, had I been another kind of person, I would have been ecstatic to have my name associated with Abbey Road, a studio where The Beatles and a lot of other great artists had recorded. But I knew that them white boys over there did not know how to mix black music. They did not know how to mix R&B music. When I found out my shit was mixed at Abbey Road, it was wrong.

I used to test my records in my car's stereo system to hear if the levels were right. When I was listening to every other hit R&B album, their level was way up here. On *Lovers Again* the levels were way down. I've got to turn the damn box all the way up for me to even appreciate the recording. I knew what had happened and it was wrong and it just made me mad. I didn't want to have nothing to do with them after that. It was over with. I didn't want to support the album, I don't want to have anything else to do with it, period. That's the way that went down.

There was another thing which pissed me off even more. After the album was finished, they put out a promotional CD or EP to go with it and there was a track of Nick Mundy singing one of the songs off the album.

Why am I'm I hearing his voice on anything? He was the producer. How did you guys let this happen? What is this? That was so unheard of, so unbelievable, that I had to distance myself from the whole thing.

Despite this experience, my friendship with Buzz Willis remained strong. It's an honour to play BB King's club in New York and whenever I perform there, Buzz is going to be there in the audience.

In 2008 I was back in the studio for the first time in six years recording a covers album, *Alex Loves*. I did the album with a really good friend of mine, Nat Augustin, and I thought it came out really well. I actually really enjoyed making this album because it was actually fun to go into the studio and sing other people's songs, putting my own style on the material.

I'd been promised by the label, EMI, that the album would receive significant TV promotion but this never materialized. Unfortunately we never got anywhere near the sales it deserved.

Despite this, I still enjoyed the experience because it had reignited my desire to get back in the studio. New material was going to keep me in the game. Truth is you never know when the little spark will generate a resurgence in your career. Whether you admit it or not, we all want that other day in the sun, that last hurrah when people can say, "Alex had a big hit record."

In this period in my life, I'd carry on performing whenever I could, taking gigs all over to keep some money coming in. One of the best experiences I had was going on tour for four months opening the show for Gladys Knight and the Pips.

I've been fortunate to be in the company of people that I can learn from and respect and Gladys is one of them. Another is Patti LaBelle and she and I have become good associates over the years. I think that I can use the word friends now.

Most of the stuff I learned, I took from females who took the time to sit down and talk to me. They'd talk about serious things in the industry, things that were going to give me longevity.

Gladys taught me a lot. We'd have different conversations and I'd ask her lots of questions. She said, "Alex, I just want to share one thing with you, it's very important. Sometimes in the industry, the bigger they are, the nicer they are."

I took that away as being the bigger you are, the nicer you should be. I think that is what she was saying. How do you maintain your dignity and your individuality, still being a star, still sharing it with your fans? By being kind, by being a good person, a nice person. Not by being the stereotype of what success in the music industry turns you into.

People say crazy things about Alexander O'Neal, but I will always get out of the car and go and greet a fan, when most people would just drive on, pull up their shit on you. I go and stop the car. Okay, I have got to do this, it's a fan. People want to talk to me coming out of the theatre taking pictures.

Security might be rushing me on, but I will always go, "Stop, I'll do this". I'm in contact with my fans all over the world, all the time. Gladys didn't have to teach me to have a heart because I have always been a kind, good person. I know the answer to the question about trying to do the right thing. When it comes to showbusiness, when it comes to my fans, I am really searching to do the right thing. And the right thing does not mean leaving fans hanging on the side of the building when they are trying to get a picture with you or trying to get an autograph. Why would you pull off with the car and leave them shitting on themselves when you could have just taken the time to get out of the car and go deal with that? How much was it going to hurt you just to get out the car and then go and sign a picture?

Theses are fans who bring copies of your albums. They are putting your albums up in your face, saying, "Please, sign this! Please!" and then you pull off. That's not being true to the idea that "the bigger they are, the nicer they are" that Gladys talked about. That's not being kind. That is not being grateful and giving back. You see, I have found that some artists can't do that. For some artists it's not in their make-up. It is within my make-up all day and all night to be a kind, good person. No situation is going to take that from me. You can't stop me from being that.

That is why Gladys has been a star and why she still does whatever she wants to do. I bet Gladys ain't done a track show – a show where you have to lip-synch to a playback of your song. Look how many track shows I had to do just to keep food on the table. I had to go out and play to playback. Superstars like myself, we ain't got no business lip-synching to our own playback. It's supposed to be a live show, every time.

Another person who I came to have a huge respect for was Bobby Z, Prince's drummer who came to me about five years after *Lovers Again* with an album project for the record company Eagle Rock.

At the time I was broke. Me and Cynthia could go through money like water so the $25,000 I was getting for what became *Saga Of A Married Man*, to date the last album I recorded, came at just the right time. I came up with the title 'cos it reflected everything that had gone on in my marriages and other failed relationships. Alexander O'Neal, Bobby Z, that one wasn't supposed to happen. I didn't know who Bobby Z was as a person. I knew his brother David Z, who was a very well-known engineer and a record producer in the Twin Cities, and also a member of Lipps, Inc. All I knew about Bobby Z was that he was somebody who you couldn't touch, somebody who was in Prince's camp. Prince knew who would be there for him and who wouldn't and Bobby Z was definitely one of the guys that would be there for him as a human being, as a man, as a brother.

To me guys in Prince's band acted like their shit don't stink. I knew they were like that. These guys walk in the building and shit on everybody just because they're in Prince's band. They walk into a building they don't give the musicians the time of day. Don't give nobody nothing other than the fact that they're stars. Now, I have got to believe that's the way that it was, because I got some of that information from Bobby Z himself.

When he came to me, I couldn't get my head around why he was doing this, producing a record with Alexander O'Neal. But I was intrigued about me having a musical relationship with him.

When we went into the studio, we invited songwriters from all over the country to submit songs to us, and we picked the best to go on the album alongside a few we'd done ourselves. Immediately, as we began working, I knew Bobby was someone I liked and could do good work with. As I got to know him, I could see he was a very kind and sensible man. Before I thought he was just one of these arrogant Jewish white boys that could cheat on everybody, because he was with Prince.

In truth, with Bobby Z, everything I asked of him on the album he delivered and at the same time he tried to make sure I was okay outside of the studio. When I needed cash advances, he'd sort it out. I know the $25,000 I was making is more money than the average Joe would ever see. But in comparison with the amounts I'd seen in the past, this ain't no money to me. See, I'd made several $25,000 mistakes in my life and I'm not talking about drugs. One time I spent that amount of money on an office for my business. But I wasn't ready to have no company. I wasn't ready to really oversee a company, give it purpose and direction. I invested $25,000 into renovating this office in Downtown Minneapolis and the doors never opened for business. Another time I handed over $10,000 in cash for 80 acres of land up in Moose Lake, Minnesota and never even got the deeds. At the time that amount of money meant nothing to me.

Saga of a Married Man was a great project. I was in control of myself. This time, there was no going into the studio high. Never, ever. I had changed. This time there was no cocaine.

While I loved Bobby Z and my time with him was a great experience, coming from some major record companies to work with Eagle Rock was a nightmare. They were a small company out of London and were synonymous with rock music. I'm like, "They're trying something new here, right? They're going over into the R&B world." But they didn't do shit for the record, okay? They did nothing, absolutely nothing for the record. I don't know if it, the whole project, was a tax write-off, or what. I still don't know today.

Saga is a great album. It has a lot of great songs, but my fans never really got to hear it. It was released but if you don't know the record's out there, how are you going to know to go and buy it? This was at the start of the social media craze. The dawn of "do everything on the internet". Eagle Rock thought they would sell the record without having to go into stores. You got to go out there and do all the leg work to sell an R&B record. You can't just put it out there. They didn't want to do that. Consequently, it was another great Alexander O'Neal album that we lost. It's like the album never existed.

CHAPTER 17
Children

After the experience of *Lovers Again*, for the first time in my life, I put music second.

I spent a lot of time in England, and I spent a lot of time in the States. I had a relationship with Cynthia that I was trying to build, and I was also trying to keep relationships with my children. I still want these relationships with the kids. I've got to keep trying. I can't quit. There were some children, a couple, who I'd basically only met once, let alone had a relationship with them. I had to work on all that shit. I wanted to let them all know that I loved them and I did care about them.

They thought I resented them, but the truth is that your father always liked you and loved you, and he never resented you.

Those five years were a time in my life when I needed to confirm some things, especially with those girls, especially in Minneapolis.

It had taken me four years to reconnect with my daughters Harmony and Alexandra and, when I did, it broke my heart. They were living in a shitty two-bedroom apartment in the ghetto part of Las Vegas. When I walked into that place, it was absolutely drop-dead filthy.

Debbie had taken my princesses and made them into hoochie mamas. Hood rats. This was the life they were living. The place where they were living was atrocious. But, now I had found them, I could help out. Debbie got a new place and I was voluntarily paying $600 a month for the girls, no court necessary, which was more money than they'd seen in a long time.

The first time Debbie sent the girls to Minneapolis to visit me, I didn't like what I found. They weren't the protected little Alexander O'Neal superstar girls who had been all over the world, to places such as Germany, Japan, England, France and all over America. They weren't those girls anymore.

They were two little ghetto rats, two little hoochie mamas who thought that they could come and sit with me and show no respect. They thought that they knew something. They didn't know shit. Couldn't talk about nothing. They had shit and didn't know shit. We tried to turn that around, Cynthia and I. We tried to turn that around, but it was hard because they didn't like us.

Remember their mother is their best friend. You don't say nothing about their mother. She could be wrong with two left shoes on her right foot but don't say nothing about their mother, period. I learned very quickly not to say anything bad about their mother, never. We barely even mentioned Debbie in their company. My concentration was on the girls.

They made Cynthia's life a whole hell, like a lot of people do to their stepmom. Especially women on women. The more Cynthia did that was beautiful and lovely for them, the more she took them places that they hadn't been to before, the more they played up. They showed Cynthia that they couldn't stand her.

It was getting to a point where I'd have to say, "You might not to be able to stand her, but you're going to have to respect her. Because she is not going anywhere. Now, if you're going to come here for the summers, for Christmas, or for holidays in her house, you are going to respect her. I know your mother didn't teach you that but she should have done."

The girls though were resenting everything that we tried to teach them.

They're getting all kinds of jewels and all kinds of material things and stuff but they're just pretending to be grateful. It's them and their mother against the world. Fuck everybody else and everything in it, even me. Fuck me. "You're my father, you're my protector – but fuck you, too. We don't have love for you like that. It's about Mom and us, we don't give a fuck. We really don't care."

We fought that for a long time, trying to have a relationship with those girls. I just did the best that I could in that situation, hoping they got something out of it.

I think, for each of my children, it's hard for them to put together the pieces of my relationship with their mother. And its sometimes hard for them accept the circumstances that brought them into this world.

While I was married to Debbie, on three occasions girls I was seeing fell pregnant. I ended up with four daughters: Faith, Cassandra and my girls Siana and Louisa whose mother was a girl called Sharon Olbekson.

Now I accept it is the responsibility of both the man and woman to take precautions if you are having sex and don't want children. To my mind, though, the greater duty lies with the woman because having unprotected sex can have lifetime consequences.

Sharon was just a girl with whom I'd never even been in the public eye with. The next thing I know she's having my kids. When she told me the news, to me it was like her saying, "I'm going to be involved with you for the rest of your life." Who the fuck said you can be in my life? I never meant you to be in my life, goddamn. You think that you going to get anything positive out of something like that when you don't even have a relationship with this guy? You barely know this motherfucker and you're going to have his baby? Oh, I guess him being Alexander O'Neal the superstar doesn't fucking hurt, does it?

The problem is that when a child from a situation like this grows up they think, "You don't like us, you don't love us." These are the kind of questions that come into play, but the truth is, while some of my children were not planned, I do love them all. But I don't see it coming back from them.

Every one of my kids treats me like shit, okay?

They have taken from me, they have extracted in every way they can. But they don't give nothing back in return, they don't give me no love. They don't even deal with me, and it's like I don't even matter. I think that I brought much more to your life than being that old drug addict, crackhead ass daddy. That crackhead ass father of yours.

But I bet you motherfuckers will call me if you need $500. I bet you will call me if you needed $5,000. I bet you would find a way to call me then won't you?

Of course, I'm always going to be there. I'm definitely going to be there for them.

I've never turned my back on any of them. I don't care what they do.

I have a mother and if I hadn't talked to her within two or three weeks I would feel like, what the fuck is wrong with me, right?

See these guys, they don't even call. They don't even think of me. And you know why? Because they don't give a shit about me. They give a shit about their mother. That's all they think about, their mother.

When these children were born, I didn't try and wriggle out of the situation and pretend I wasn't the father.

You get yourself in those kind of situations, and you've got to be truthful about it. The kids are yours, you ain't going to lie. If you lie then you are a punk. If you were to look at yourself in the mirror, what you'd see is a goddamn liar. A coward. Someone who is afraid to step up to the plate and take on responsibility.

I have never been a conventional father in any sense of the word, and I have always told that to my kids. Our life may not be like the white picket fence and the dog and the cat all that shit, not like that. This is showbusiness, this is singing, this is the hardcore showbusiness life here. That's the life that I am living and it's not going to go away just because you were born. Sorry.

Kids, you have to get used to my lifestyle and I have to get used to yours, okay?

Some of them are paying me back, I guess, for me not being there, for not being their conventional father. Well, get the fuck over it. Get over it. I do love you, and I do care about you. You're not going to be able to stop that. You can't take it away from me. You can't make me not love you because I'm going to love every one of you like we were raised in the same house together.

I deserve much more than that from them, but they don't see it. That's fine. I'll get over it. I'm a big boy. I'm a grown man and I will get on with my life. I'm not going to spend my life worrying, having my heart hurt because my kids don't have enough respect for what I brought to their life to even call me. They don't even call me on Father's Day. Fuck my birthday. I don't give a shit about that because I don't give a shit about birthdays. But Father's Day? How could you have a Father's Day and have a father and not call him? That's crazy to me. That's disrespectful. Now, the rest of the shit can go to hell but Father's Day? I bet you will call your mother on Mother's Day and I bet you will be trying to be something special. My kids never sent me no goddamn gifts.

Some of them are living in the past in respect to their father, the relationship that we have. They should accept that they don't have a monopoly on not having a father being in the house all day. Letting some things go from the past, growing up and forming or having a great relationship with your father now, that's what adults do. That's what grown-ups do and that's what real responsible people do.

If I had shown them anything and given them anything, the burden is not for me to come over there and try to have a relationship with you. It's for you to demand of yourself and say, "I'm not going to accept anything less than having a relationship with the person that wants to have a relationship with me, who happens to be my father." Do I want to have a great relationship with my daughters? Yes, I do. I'd love to have a great relationship.

I'm here for all of them. I'm a grown man, I'm a responsible grown man and I'm your father and I will never leave you. I will never turn my back on my kids, any of them. They've turned their back on me, a lot of them, but I will never turn my back on them and they can take that to the bank.

One thing that has helped me in dealing with all this is the fact God has always been in my life. He's been a part of my conversation, a part of my being, everything. I think that's one of the things that got me out of some of the bad shit that I've placed myself inside.

I've tried to teach all my kids about God, the power of God.

I don't care if you can be perceived as the baddest person on the planet. You can still come back with God at all times. I always kept that inside of me, and I always tried to teach my son, my girls, about the power of prayer. Because I know this thing to be true. There is a God and He does exist and He has a plan.

Through all of my bad-boy shit, I always kept God in my life, because there was always good in me. The one daughter I have really struggled with is Cassandra who I had with another girlfriend who, like my wife, was called Deborah. After she'd had Cassandra and we'd stopped seeing each other, Deborah had married a white guy, with whom she had two more kids. Cassandra grew up in this white family, with two white brothers. And there she was, of mixed race, more dark-skinned than I am. I guess it was a lot to deal with.

When she was about 15 years old, I reached out to her to see if she wanted a relationship with me. At first, she wasn't ready. She knew I was trying to get a hold of her. I've tried to bring her to my home, to bring her into the family thing with the girls and everybody else, but she didn't want to come.

I did manage to talk to her on a few occasions and at one point I even set up a session in a recording studio for her. I was going to help her because she's a great singer and songwriter, she can sing her ass off. She's more talented than any of the other girls. The first time I heard her sing, I actually cried.

I've got about four girls whose voices are off the scale but they don't have the other stuff that it takes to go and be a star. First of all, in order to be a star, you've got to want it. You can't just want it because you see it on TV. That's like blindly wanting something you don't have any knowledge about. You just think you do but you just see all that stuff and say, "I want that." But they are not willing to go through what it takes to get that. If anybody has the knowledge and knows how to get there it would be me.

At the end of the day, though, every time I tried to help Cassandra, she wouldn't follow my lead. I don't understand how with a guy like me, her father, who has been all over the world and achieved so much in the R&B industry, she wouldn't follow my guidance. I'm telling her she had 100 per cent of nothing and I am giving her 50 per cent of something. I can't guarantee her that she could get a career, but I can guarantee that she will get heard by the most important people in the industry. Even if she got turned down, I can guarantee that she will get turned down by the best. I can guarantee that. I can guarantee the right people will hear this shit. We won't get turned down by some guy who doesn't even matter.

When you have people like Jimmy Jam and Terry in your corner, other great producers, you don't know what you can do. But Cassandra disappeared off the face of the earth. She sent me the nastiest letter I've ever seen, and I sent it back to her. I've seen her since on different occasions and I hope, one day, that we can have a relationship. At the moment, though, I guess she's in what one of my other daughters calls the "Hate Dad Club".

What can you do with something like that? You can't do shit. I had the same with my son Carlton. We were supposed to record this father/son song and he just vanished. I've tried to pass the torch on but they turned their backs on me.

Today I am just going to get on with my own life. I'm 63. Who knows how much time there is left for me in God's plan?

CHAPTER 18
Cynthia

As you've seen, I've had many women in my life, but as you'd expect, I've kept the full story of the best one 'til last.

If you've ever seen the movie *The Best Little Whorehouse in Texas*, you may remember the opening scene where there's this fantastic pair of legs. Well, they belong to my wife, Cynthia.

On her path to meeting me, Cynthia was having her own success. She was a local Minneapolis girl and a really voluptuous woman. She was a winner of the Miss Burnsville title, one of the more prestigious beauty pageants held in the Twin Cities and her looks were destined to catch my eye.

Before our paths crossed, however, she had set out on her own career as a dancer. Her mentor was Carlton Johnson who was a star on *The Carol Burnett Show* and had done stuff like choreograph The Temptations and Michael Jackson's *The Wiz*. Carlton also choreographed the movie *The Blues Brothers* and, through him, Cynthia landed a part as a dancer – the only white girl in the troupe.

When she came to me to audition for the Wembley Arena dates, it only took me a few minutes to know she was perfect for the show.

I knew I liked her when I first saw her. I was attracted to her, but I'm the boss. I needed her respect her more than hitting on her. It was that kind of shit.

We started the tour and one night I don't know what got into me, but on stage, I went to stand behind Cynthia and sang the line

"I found my woman" looking right into her eyes, very serious. She told me later that she was flustered because, up until that point, I had hardly said two words to her.

We didn't talk about it or anything but I would kind of place myself in her presence when I could. If I knew the band was at the bar, I would pop down just so I could see her.

After the tour ended, we were back in Minneapolis and, after the row over the $50,000 she'd given away, Debbie had walked out on me taking the girls with her to Florida. I had no idea if she'd be back so, after about six weeks, I called Cynthia on the phone at her apartment. I said a bunch of us were going down to a club – would she like to join us?

She said she couldn't go as she was already in bed.

I called again another night, and this time she agreed to join us down town at the Whitney Hotel. I made sure there were people around so it wouldn't look like I was just trying to hit on her but it must have been pretty obvious why I was interested. I'd hired a suite complete with a whirlpool which was the size of a small swimming pool. Cynthia walked in looking like a million dollars, but it quickly became clear that she wasn't even going to let me kiss her let alone anything else. I wasn't put off. What it did was make me more determined to be with her.

She told me she had a boyfriend and that, if she was going to be with me, she would have to end that relationship before she could start up with me. She was the kind of person who does things properly. My respect for her went up a million per cent.

I ended up giving the keys to the suite to a friend and telling him, "Happy birthday, have a ball." I went back to my house alone, put on some Sinatra and Mel Tormé and thought about what my next move could be.

I had to go away for a few weeks for a mini tour and when I came back decided it was time to act – I was going to call Cynthia and if she didn't say what I needed to hear then I wasn't going to mess with her, it would be game over, I'd have nothing to do with her.

I went on the phone with this stupid attitude, saying. "I bet you didn't do what you said and break it off with your guy, did you?"

Cynthia immediately shut me down. "How would you know? You never even called all this time you were away. As it happens, I did break it off."

That was when I knew we were on, that I could begin courting her properly.

At this point, I was living at home with the boys, my nephew Roe, Jamaican Jessie who was doing the housekeeping and cooking, and my boy Mac who was my right-hand man, who I trust to this day with anything I have.

I asked Cynthia to come by the house and I'm thinking, "Yes, now this shit's going to be on," and told the boys to make themselves scarce. I wanted the house to myself for when Cynthia turned up. When she arrived, I can remember she was wearing this rust-coloured jumpsuit which showed off her amazing figure, all curvy like an old Coke bottle.

I had on a pair of biker shorts and a tank top with food all over it and I'm thinking I'm really *GQ* smooth.

We talked and we kicked it that day – that's where it started.

A few weeks later, Debbie came back. But I never got rid of Cynthia.

Debbie became aware of her not long after we moved to Vegas and I had to go back to Minneapolis to attend some drug treatment ordered by the court. I moved in with Cynthia and Debbie knew I was there and seemed fine with it.

Cynthia didn't bring anything but positivity into my life. Every time I saw her my whole world lit up. Every time I was with her I was blessed, thanking God for giving her to me. She had everything that I could want in a woman. From the top of her head to the bottom of her feet, she is the total package. She was then and, for me, she always will be.

When I was on the phone one time talking to Debbie back in Vegas, Debbie overheard me say to Cynthia, "I love you". Now, for your wife to hear you tell another woman you love her ain't cool, and I tried to make out I'd never said it. But she didn't believe me and asked me to give Cynthia up. I am at the point where I had so much anger in my heart, so much resentment against Debbie, that whole thing from Wembley, that at the end of the day I didn't care what she felt. Period.

Debbie had destroyed the total trust I had in her. She destroyed every ounce of it.

Cynthia was the first woman I had given that trust to again. There was a special place in my heart, of purity, which Cynthia had entered.

Just how special she was I saw when the FBI raided my house and took all my money. Cynthia went out and somehow got together $13,000 for me which, along with some cash from other friends, got me through. After that, I knew I was never going to give Cynthia up. She'd been there for me when I needed her most.

It may seem hard to understand, but I still loved Debbie very much, I was still married to her and we had two lovely babies who were my heart. Everything that I had was still hers.

I knew in my heart that, if a woman leaves you, especially if she's already given you two or three trials runs, one of these times she's going to leave you for good.

I was always looking for a woman I could be with, but Cynthia is the woman I can't be without. She is that rock for me. In all the relationships I have ever had in my life Cynthia has made me a better man than I ever thought I could be. My love has always been pure for Cynthia. It has always been just her and me. We have been together for 29 years now, and I was right not to give her up when Debbie asked me to.

I knew, one of those times, that Debbie was going to leave me. One of those times she walked out would be for real, and she wasn't going to stay with me forever. If I'm being honest, she didn't have a lot of reason to stay. I can't sit here and put it all on her. She didn't have a lot of reasons to stay as a woman, and there were a lot of extenuating circumstances for her to deal with. I was determined never to give her my love after all that Wembley stuff. That situation was done.

But the girls, they were my life.

If I had been a smart man, I would have just divorced Debbie and had a relationship with my girls and that would have been the end of all Debbie's troubles and all of mine at the same time

Truth is I would never give Debbie up, I would never turn my back on her, walk away from her, ever. I would never do that. I would never have left Debbie in a billion years. Even though I loved Cynthia to the maximum, I would never give Debbie up to be with her. You know why? Because this is my family and family comes first before any damn thing. If you can work something out you do that. But I never got that opportunity with Debbie. I was never given the chance to work anything out because Debbie cheated on me. She walked out and took the girls with her.

People don't understand the trauma that you go through in that parting stage. All of the dreams and premonitions I'd had about Debbie – all the things that I imagined she was doing and the kind of people that she was around – well, I was exactly motherfucking right. She was running around with people I'd never associate with, having my daughters around all these unstable non-achievers.

After she left, for four years I'd wake up out of dead sleeps with these types of thoughts. The pain that I felt in my heart was absolutely phenomenal. I am still working to get rid of that shit today. I wonder why this comes back after all these years but it never goes away. I repeat: I would never have left Debbie in a billion years.

I have always felt as long as I don't know about a third party, don't see it, don't hear about it, what grown-ups do is their business. It wouldn't be an issue. No one is excluded from that, not even my family.

The difference is when you find out your partner is unfaithful. When I finally found out Debbie was with another married man in Vegas, it was all over. There was nothing left to talk about.

Even when Debbie left, I didn't immediately hook up with Cynthia. She came out to visit me in Vegas a few times but it was some while before I eventually went back to Minneapolis and we moved in together for real and we've been together ever since. Everything we have encountered, every success, we have achieved together.

Before Cynthia, I admit I wasn't a good husband at all. I was just a good provider and I thought that gave me the right to be dominant over any woman. I never had the respect for women, not until Cynthia.

She taught me how to maintain a relationship. There's two rules of thumb, "Don't beat her and don't cheat her." Cynthia is the type of woman who is not going to deal with a third party. It's not going to happen. She doesn't deal with that kind of shit. At the beginning Cynthia put up with a lot of my shit, other women too, don't get me wrong. But she quickly made it clear she wasn't going to tolerate it. Period. Either I was going to straighten up and treat her right, treat our marriage right, or it wasn't going to be. At least I got the option to say, "Is she important enough to me for me to straighten up or do I keep trying to pull the wool over her eyes?"

I never had this kind of conversation with Debbie. If I had, I probably would have listened, that's how much I loved her.

Today it is Cynthia or nothing. I have told her that. If anything happened in our relationship, I will never be in another relationship with a woman again. This is the last one for me.

CHAPTER 19

Big Brother is watching you

In 2015 the producers of the British version of *Celebrity Big Brother* contacted me and asked if I'd like to be on the show. I knew all about the programme and absolutely hated it, but knew it would present a great opportunity for me to raise my profile, put myself in front of an entirely new audience and make them aware of my music and what I've achieved over the years.

I had no illusions about how the show would be, that the producers would be in control of everything and everybody and I thought I was prepared for that. As it turned out, the way they manipulated everything was beyond anything I imagined.

The night we all entered the *Big Brother* house I got a hell of a rush from the reaction of the crowd. I was wearing a suit and my tennis shoes which is something you see in New York all the time, but for some reason, the British audience made such a fuss out of the way I was dressed.

The first feeling I had inside the house was of being incarcerated. I understand the need for *Big Brother* to be in control, but feeling imprisoned was uncomfortable. Everything had locks on it. It was like being in jail. I didn't like the couple of times that I spent in a lock-up, so I already knew it was going to be a test. I don't like being locked up and I hate surprises.

But one thing, after getting in there and finding my way around, I have to say that the *Big Brother* staff took very good care of us. They were very attentive with everything, especially the alcohol in the evening.

I think everybody, three-quarters of people in there it appeared to me, were very agitated when we had the red light on. The red light meant that you can't go into the room with the fridge, the booze and the stuff. But when that green light went on, boy, you could see people jumping up. "John, John, John. Have a drink! Have this, that and the other."

I think that *Celebrity Big Brother* knew you can't take everything away from people like that. Being locked up like that together is going to bring out the edges. For the people who didn't drink, it made it much better for the people who did because we had much more. It really helped you go to your bed, kept your anxiety level down. That was my biggest thing.

Once we'd settled in we all knew that we had to get through this thing the best way we could. There were a lot of annoying factors, as *Big Brother* puts all these obstacles in your way to push your buttons. Some of those situations the viewers see, some of them have been spurred on by *Big Brother* the way they have moved, setting things up.

You have 57 cameras on you. You have TV producers and psychologists watching your behaviour, seeing who can get their buttons pushed the most.

One of the housemates was Perez Hilton and, from the outset, a lot of us thought he was a plant, someone put in the house just to stir things up.

When I first started to get to know him, he struck me as somebody that I didn't want to be friends with or involved with because he was a shit stirrer. I think he gets a thrill out of being hated. You know guys like that: they have neither fame nor real talent. In a reality show, he could take the most loved role or the most hated, he wouldn't care because that's it. He's so hungry for celebrity status but he'll never get it validated through that type of behaviour.

I had a big thing of trying to get people to see the show for what it was. "Guys, we really don't live here. You're really not my family. This is really a television show. You're all going to believe it, this is entertainment. That's all it is."

In a situation like we were in, there was always going to be tensions.

Nadia Sawalha, I found, was a very two-faced bitch. Keith Chegwin, oh God, that guy was absolutely pathetic to me. First of all, he would do anything for the money. That's number one and secondly, he never makes a decision about anything. He was always thinking, "I've got to be this perfect British guy who everybody likes." He's not that nice. Underneath he's a sneaky, sly little snake in the grass. He just pretends like he's a nice guy. That's his role.

I got on with Katie Hopkins out of all the people in the house. We had a row early on in the show but, once we'd got that out of the way, she understood me very well and I understood her and we also found we liked each other. I never expected to have a relationship with her like that. To me, out of all the women in the house, I respected her the most and I thought she was a very kind person with a very kind heart. I think the public will never know what kind of heart Katie Hopkins really has because all they're going to see is what she triggers out there. She's paid to be the bad girl and she does it very well.

Another housemate was the singer Kavana, whom I'd never heard of before going into the show. As I got to know him I thought yes, I like him, we're cool.

The whole *Big Brother* experience, in fact, the one thing about these kind of situations, is that if you ever thought you were a liberal person, it will test you. Now, let's see how liberal you really are.

With all these gay people around me and me being a heterosexual man, I didn't find it difficult. I've been around gay people in the industry. That doesn't scare me. But I never wanted to get so close that I could see stuff that I didn't really want to see or don't want to know. I don't want to know anything, and I don't want to see anything. I don't want to experience anything that you guys are doing because that's your thing. Everybody has their own opinion, like I said. I don't hate people because of their sexual preferences or their nationalities, whatever. I don't believe in that because I was raised differently, raised not to hate and that takes a pretty special kind of person.

On *Celebrity Big Brother*, I was conscious from the start that I needed to be aware of how I would be perceived outside. I had already decided, when I walked through the doors, that I was just going to be Alex. I didn't have to build a character. Everything you see is Alexander O'Neal, all day, every day. Pretty much a guy who's going to tell you, "If you think that you're right and I know that you're wrong, I'm going to tell you if it's in reference to me or my things."

The one housemate who was putting on an act and was a *Big Brother* plant was Perez and we all felt it. See, it's okay to be obnoxious and all this stuff but he's downright nasty and disgusting. His nastiness would make a person like me, who has a certain amount of intelligence on a good day, wonder, "If he is that nasty and this is natural, how nasty is he really? Screwing the window and licking the window and doing all kinds of repulsive things, then I'm around a person who's really fucked up."

I said to him one time, "Perez you need to keep your mouth shut, man. You're always starting some shit. You're always starting shit. What is it with you?"

Viewers who watched the show will know Perez tried to wind me up, blowing me kisses, standing over me while I was in bed and deliberately breathing all over my food. I tried to stay the fuck away from him. I tried to stay away from him because I thought, "You're never going to make me hit you." A lot of the cats when I got out of the show they said, "Man, I would have done this and I would have done that."

Of course, it all came to a head when I finally lost my temper and said he had a "faggot look" on his face.

I was called to the Big Brother Diary Room and, minutes later, *Big Brother* announced to the house that I had decided to quit the show.

Bullshit. I had made up my mind, at that point, that I was on my way to make Perez's life a holy hell. Just like what he was doing to everybody else, I was slowly doing my own thing to him. I'm following him, and I'm stalking him and saying, "Walk around. Put your dress on." I was like, "I want to stay within my lane, but I'm going to stalk you. I want to see how good you really are. How much can you take? You're blowing kisses at me, playing games. You and *Big Brother* are trying to push my buttons. I know what you are doing. Coming up by my bed coughing like that and pretending like that and then go back to your bed and whispering "Big Brother, it's working. It's working." So I said, "Okay, I am going to flip that on you. Now, how are you going to handle this black man constantly following you around, harassing you all day, every day, starting shit with you? How do you handle it?"

I wanted to scare him because he knew that, in America, he would not harass or even look at me funny. Out on the street, in the real world, you want to stop a black man in America? You want to play games with him, and beg that he don't kill you? You know that's not accepted. Perez, you know, you can't do that.

Now you see that I am not playing with you anymore. I am going to show these cats what kind of pumpkin you really are. At that point *Big Brother* picked up on it and I was called me to the Diary Room. I never knew when I got there that I wasn't going back down into the house, that it was already decided that I was done.

I can't remember exactly what they said but the way they explained it was, "You've done great. Your profile for ten days, it was great. That was great. We don't want you to blow that prog-ress. We've talked to you and we think it's time. It's finished for you, okay?"

Truth is *Big Brother* was worried they were no longer in control. They were used to manoeuvring everything but now it was becoming the Alexander O'Neal and Perez Hilton show. They were not going to have that kind of thing. It was too intense for them. They couldn't control it.

They weren't directly throwing me out. But they wanted me to agree to call it a day while, at the same time, they wanted to portray it that I had decided to walk. Bizarrely they said that if it was my choice to walk they wouldn't pay me the fee for appearing in the show. I'd only get the full amount by agreeing to be fired and keeping my mouth shut about what had gone down.

When I finally came out of the house, I was glad I had done it. I had a chance to show a lot of different aspects of myself and gained a lot of new fans as well, so that was a really, really great thing.

I've accepted the fact that *Celebrity Big Brother* defined a chapter in my life but that doesn't define my life as a whole. What I do is I'm a singer. I do shows and that's what I do for a living. That's what I've been doing for more than 30 years. I was able to put *Big Brother* behind me very quickly other than the fame from it. I enjoyed that part of it.

On Christmas Day, 2016, I was sitting at home when a trailer came on for this year's series of *Big Brother*. Then the news broke that George Michael had died.

Back in the day, George and I were good friends and spent many a night together at Browns nightclub in London. Now I respected George a lot but to me, despite his hit records, it seemed he had never done anything of real significance, that put a stamp on who George was as a singer and musician and why he was considered so important. Other than Wham! he had some records which were kinda legendary but I didn't see anything significant which could identify George as a standout, iconic performer. Out of all the things that he tried, all the collaborations, what do you actually remember him for? Some Wham! songs? Singing with Elton John? Performing at the Freddie Mercury concert? For me, there's no real body of work there which identifies him with the likes of say, Stevie Wonder, Michael Jackson or Amy Winehouse – those types of megastars.

What hurt me the most about his passing was the thought he may have been about to have that late day in the sun that we all chase.

I'd heard he was getting his shit together and was curious to see where he was going to go as a singer. Was he going to come up and reclaim the throne, have a hit album and the massive career all over again? He was primed and ready to be the man, and the world was his oyster.

I have been very fortunate in my career to meet all kinds of people, some like George who I could call my friend. I've worked with some incredible people, the A team, and to have their respect and be recognized as a great R&B singer is phenomenal.

One of the more interesting people I worked with was Jilly Goolden, the British wine critic and TV presenter. We met on the programme *Celebrity Wife Swap* where I got to stay with her for a week while Cynthia moved in with Jilly's husband, Paul.

Before we did the programme, I had no idea who Jilly was but was really looking forward to meeting her. When filming began, I quickly discovered we were as different as night and day. We had totally different philosophies on everything. About the only thing we agreed on was having respect for others. I don't think Jilly had ever been around someone who spoke and behaved like I did. Where I am animated and emotional, she is quiet and more sensible.

The whole time we were making the programme we had someone from the production team living with us, kinda like a chaperone, making sure nothing crazy happened. Of course, nothing crazy was ever going to go down. The only problem I had was that I wasn't going to give up on my weed during the time we were making the programme. So, whenever I felt like a smoke, I'd take my bike out and go off to a park for a couple of hours and chill out.

As with *Big Brother*, I was very conscious while making this programme that the viewers saw exactly what sort of man I am. I didn't want to put on this fake "white black man" persona, nicely spoken, pretend manners. I didn't want to be no Chris Eubank motherfucker, the whitest black Brit I have ever seen in my whole goddamn life. I wanted to be true to myself, be the real me because that's one of the things I've discovered, as a black American living in the UK, the Brits love you to be yourself. The more true to yourself you are, the more you are going to be accepted. So long as Alexander O'Neal stays real, the love affair continues.

Some of the fans I have in Britain have been so loyal, so down with me. I don't have that in America. In the States, I don't have the same people following me around, coming to all my shows. In Britain I'll ask my fans, "Why do you come to all the shows, some 200 times, hearing all the same songs?" And you know what they say? "Because every night is a different night. You might think you're singing the same songs but every night you're different."

This is what helps keep me real. After 40-odd years in the industry, I've figured out what my responsibility is, to continue to perform and make people feel good, to have a great time.

In the years since I was filling out Wembley Arena and the Hammersmith Odeon, I've played countless small venues all over the UK and all the time I've had a ball.

When it comes to my job, I don't differentiate where I play. Every night my mission is to perform as the best Alexander O'Neal I can be. Whether it's a little pub in Liverpool or Leicester, a shitty club with a fucked up sound system, I don't care, they'll get the same performance, the Alex that wants to do well, wants to win.

Of course, there are nights when you can arrive at a venue in a fucked up mood but you have to put that away, get on with the job.

Looking back over my career I know that I have been blessed to be able to make singing my livelihood. Shit, a little dirt-poor kid from Natchez, Mississippi, who has found all this fame, all this fortune through singing songs. Imagine I went for a real job and they asked, "What have you been doing for the last 40 years?"

"Well, I've been singing. I'm an entertainer."

"Really? We'll give you a call back."

Shit, today I probably couldn't even get a job pumping gas.

CHAPTER 20

My destiny

In my years of success, I've seen millions of dollars slip into and out of my hands. Yet I don't regret a single thing I've done. Life's for living, not watching it pass you by.

But, as I look back on my career and the people who have lived off my success, it does leave a slightly bitter taste that the cake didn't get shared evenly.

Take my greatest hits album released by Tabu/Virgin in 2004. It got to number 12 in the UK chart and went gold in just two weeks and yet I didn't get a quarter. They took all the money. Of course, it's okay all that stuff is coming back, but I've got to make some decisions at some point in time. Do I want to ruffle some feathers to get my money?

I've always said that the record companies did a lot of good things for me, but they did not share the wealth. They kept all the money, and that's wrong. I don't even want to know how many millions of dollars they've had while, in comparison, the likes of myself and Cherrelle – we never got a quarter. They never gave us a dime.

They gave us a lot and gave us the best of themselves, and I will always be grateful for that. But they also rolled our career like a witch riding your back. They rolled our career until they didn't want to ride anymore.

Jimmy Jam, Terry Lewis and Tabu records, all these entities: when they collected those cheques, they never told us how much money they were getting off of us, our songs. They moved to collect these cheques and we were collecting nothing. We were collecting zero.

I'm being honest here and I know it may upset people, especially Terry. Every time I have ever needed Terry, he's always been there. Any time I have asked him for a loan or anything, I pay him back. Because one thing I can't stand is for somebody who borrows from me – comes and gets something from me and don't pay me back – it drives me crazy. All I want to see is integrity. I want to see if you come to me and take a loan, you need me, I'm there for you, you pay me back.

Don't think about how to pay it through some work or through some recording. You pay me back like I gave you. If I gave you cash, you give cash back. That's what Terry and I do. So, I maintain my integrity with him. He's always been there when I needed him. I still love you, T, it's not going to alter the past. But you guys took all the money and we didn't get a quarter. We sang our asses off and you got the best of us. Even at this late date, it's not too late to make amends.

I do feel like this and there is nothing wrong with that. I have every right to feel like this.

Here's my take on it. I've made a lot of money in my career. Had I been a different kind of person I would have millions and millions right now. I'm not worried about money now, but I always stay concerned about it because I have always been a working-class artist so I'm always on point about taking care of my family. I have had enough in my career to be a millionaire five times over.

There are millionaires out there who started their journey to being a millionaire with much less than I've seen. They've not been in the same position that I was in.

Truth is, I never did want to be no millionaire. I just wanted to be able to work when I want without worrying about making the next big pay day. Being a millionaire comes along with a millionaire responsibility. That was never me and I don't regret it.

I don't think I am saying anything nasty about any of these people, period. But the reality is when they examine what went down yes, categorically Alex, Cherrelle and others were done wrong in reference to the distribution of the wealth.

They could have, in their hearts, in their spirits, in their minds, they could have given us something. But they never gave us anything. We were too close to a family for them to take all the money and not share it with us, right? Right. They could have looked at each other and said, "You know what, dawg, come on, man. We got to give them a little something, man. We got to get on this stuff for we were able to use them to get to this level."

What is that about? I don't know. That's not something Alexander O'Neal would do. Put the shoes on my foot and guess what you are going to get. I'm going to hand them the money because I could not sleep at night knowing that I took all your money. I took all the money off of your voice and didn't give you any back. Sorry, I couldn't sleep at night.

After this long journey from Natchez, people will ask where am I today, how is my life?

Firstly I want to make it clear I have no regrets about the life I've lived. God gave me a gift, which brought me fame and fortune. The millions of dollars have gone but having wealth never really bothered me. Lack of money did and still does, but not the need to have more money than I could ever spend.

I have a great support system in family and friends especially Cynthia who has meant everything for me, man. She's the reason why I'm here today. Without her I might have given the press what they really thought they were going to get, and that was my demise. Sometimes it breaks my heart when I can see people thinking, "That's not fair on the dead, he's still living, goddamn it. I thought he'd long since be gone."

I've been on the death list for at least 30 years. I've been on death watch. If I'd died people would pretend like they would be shocked but they wouldn't be.

I'm not the first person who's been an addict and been famous. I don't have a monopoly on that. I'm sorry, there have been many before me and there will be many after me. That's some negative shit that comes along with the territory, the music industry. You start out being fun, it's a party. Then it becomes a habit and then it becomes a fucking job.

I found out, in my experience, that a lot of people have professed that they are clean when they know that they're not. That's just disgusting to me and I don't do that. I won't compromise. I'm not going to tell you if I'm clean or dirty, that's my business.

My drug addiction, I don't explain it and don't have to exonerate myself to any human being for my demons and my shortcomings, I won't do it. Unfortunately, drug addiction is easy to get into but it's a bitch getting out of, especially if you're a long-term user like I am. My addiction is between God and me and nobody else. Not even my children, not my wife, not anybody because they can't do shit.

They can't save me. The only person that can save me is, first of all, me. It's being alone with God, that's why I maybe get to live another day. I already figured out that like Prince says, "Life is just a party and parties weren't meant to last." As I get older, I begin to realize that I've been partying for 62 years now.

Getting old doesn't worry me because I am enjoying a great life. I have enjoyed a great life but not without a bunch of perils. There has always been bunch of things that I have had to deal with.

What scares me today is I don't know how to fill the 'hole' I feel in my life. I can do all this good shit and still have the fucking hole, that's the amazing thing about me. But I know I could do even better if I didn't have the hole. I'd be a better man, a better son to my mother, a better father to my children.

I recently lost my first cousin, Clarence Bear Anderson Jr. He was the same age as me and we were really tight, hanging out together in Natchez. He knew he wasn't well and got up and drove himself to the hospital at three o'clock in the morning. Shortly afterwards he died. That fucked me up.

Here's my cousin. He went to prison for seven years. He came out and never touched drugs again. He was a hardcore Christian, the whole nine yards. I'm still living, but where's he? He's dead. At this point in time, I can't seem to get my head around doing things to prolong my life.

I do want to get it right but, when you're a long-term drug user, it takes quite some time before you get back into society and deal with life on life's terms. I know you need to put as much into getting clean as you did getting fucked up. To get to the position where I can just say no to drugs, that would be beautiful. I know that to get there you will be in a battle every day 'til the day you die. There are people I have talked to who have been clean for 25 years and still crave it. The only thing that stops them doing it is they know if they have one they are going back, all the way.

I don't know if I should overload myself with expectations of what it would be like to be totally sober and straight, because it is fucking overwhelming to me.

I know we don't have a lot of time on this earth and I am squandering my life when I could be doing better, doing something for others.

I deal with reality every day. Do I want to be a 'normal' human after all these years? Yes. But is there a serious price to pay? Hell, yes.

Sometimes it hurts me that I have to use the best of me to exist. I am a warrior and I have to fight this satanic battle every goddamn day, not to let Satan win the war, constantly asking God to stand with me.

Without God I would have been dead a long time ago. Nobody can do that many drugs, that much shit. It's a God thing. I am a big fuck up but I recognize His kindness, Him letting me still be here. I am thankful every day. Is it a fight? Yeah, of course it's a fucking fight. Sometimes, if you are a drug addict, that fight gets overwhelming. Over-fucking-whelming. See, I don't know how to quit, how to quit on life. Once an addict, always an addict.

Do I want to be a success story? Fuck yeah. Do I want overcoming drugs to be one of my claims to fame? Fuck yes, I want it. The question now is how bad to I want it and how much am I willing to sacrifice, to endure.

My idea of being sober is always going to involve smoking some weed and having an occasional drink if I want to. In the future, I hope to get to a point where I can be around people who are offering me cocaine and I can just say no. Then I know I will be where I want to be. I know I will never be past it, just that I have succeeded in living my life without it. With all the destruction that drugs bring to your life, you have to decide what you want. Do you want the possibility of what this life can offer for happiness, or do you want the certainty of the negativity drugs will bring? It's your choice.

As you get older, you see your body being torn down by the drugs. You see the destruction that it brings to your life. You see your body responding to what you have given it.

These are my daily issues, and I want to get it right. I don't know what it is going to take but I know I am not going to quit, I am going to keep trying and keep going. Just as much as I have to keep trying in life and I am going to keep trying to conquer all my demons. I know with the help of God the possibilities of me getting it right are very good.

It scares me sometimes that I don't want to take God's love, His patience and kindness for granted 'cos we, as human beings, can easily do that. We can get complacent with where we are at in life.

I am trying to complete the journey and find that place that is going to make me happy. I hope and pray I can make it.

What comes next?

Today I live most of my time in London. Minneapolis and Saint Paul is a big metropolis but it doesn't suit my life. It makes me lazy. It's why I don't fuck around there that much. That's probably a good thing too, 'cos a lot of people in the Twin Cities area knew how talented I was but I don't think a lot of people really liked me because I was too fucking opinionated. I don't think that I got that tag because I was difficult to work with, I was just a guy that you just couldn't control, I don't want anybody telling me shit.

This year, 2017, I've got a nationwide tour booked, and I'm back in the studio.

The novelty in making and promoting an album has never gone away. I love touring, I love being out on the road and being independent. I know how much money I make and I know what to do with my family. I know where my money is going, so first of all I don't have to depend on anybody, anything period, because I'm a working man. That's what I consider myself, as a working-class entertainer. I work. I meet people on the streets of London all the time who ask me, "Do you still sing?" I should ask them, "Do you still breathe air?" That would be a better.

Singing, performing – that's what I do, all day. Everybody gets a turn, if you're blessed enough to get a chance to be in the limelight. When you're younger that's your time to shine. Some artists get in the limelight all their whole career, artists like Tom Jones and Tony Bennett. There's a built-in need for what they do. These kind of artists grow up with you, grow old with you. I'm just thankful to God that here it is, almost 40 years later, and I'm still doing the same thing. I have achieved everything that I once set out to achieve in my childhood, in my life. The things I wanted to do for my mother, I've achieved those things. These are the most important things like buying her a house and making sure that she had nice comfort and security.

My job now enables me once again to be there for my mother who's 85 years old. It enables me to be her foundation, her backbone everyday. My job is still giving me that. I'm still getting that scene. How many people can say that?

I am so thankful and so blessed. I've done everything I wanted to do.

Acknowledgements

Few of us in life know where the road is going to take us. Growing up in the 1960s in America's Deep South – a black kid in a world split apart by racial hatred – who knew what lay in store for me? My family had nothing, just the love of our mother Dora and the knowledge that life was for living, a gift not to be wasted. God had given me another gift too, a voice that would take me to a whole other world. Along the way there was joy and heartbreak, fame and despair.

There's an army of people who were with me on my journey. Many are in this book but chief among them and to whom I owe so much are Cherrelle, Jimmy Jam, Terry Lewis and Clarence Avant. Today they are joined by Steve Mottershead, who is guiding my career. These people have always been there for me when others doubted me and hated my success.

Thank you to Eugene for taking me on this journey and guiding me through the ups and downs so professionally.

For my children who know some of my story when you read this remember, Dad loves you and will always be there for you. That's what a Dad does.

To my wife Cynthia there simply aren't enough words. You taught me how to be the man I needed to be.

I never knew my father after whom I was named. God took him just before I came into the world. When we catch up down the road some time, I'll have some story to tell you.

Index